ACTING UP

Lucilla,

Joy! Love! Live!

BK

Acting Up

Winning in Business and Life Using Down-Home Wisdom

JANICE BRYANT HOWROYD

LIONCREST
PUBLISHING

ACTING UP

Winning in Business and Life Using Down-Home Wisdom

ISBN   978-1-5445-0456-8 *Hardcover*
       978-1-5445-0455-1 *Paperback*
       978-1-5445-0457-5 *Ebook*
       978-1-5445-0458-2 *Audiobook*

Elretha and John Bryant taught me more than anyone else about everything that matters. The principles they engaged raising my ten siblings and me are the same principles I have worked to engage in the growth of my organization. My husband Bernie and I pray that we've instilled these same principles as life guides for our children, Katharyn and Brett. For this, I thank them and dedicate this book to Mommie and Dad.

Contents

Prologue

THE JUMBO JET LUMBERED SLOWLY DOWN THE taxiway at Los Angeles International Airport. It turned left and then left again onto the runway. The roar of four engines rose to full thrust, accelerating the wide-body airplane down the runway faster and faster. The nose came up, and I heard the rumble of the wheels clearing the tarmac and retracting into the bay behind my seat. I craned my neck to look out of the window at the Pacific Ocean sparkling two thousand feet below. Gently, the plane banked right. We had arrived—first class from LA to Monte Carlo.

I was the CEO of a successful and growing business. But this was the first time I had ever flown first class. An organization that was honoring the top fifty female entre-preneurs in the world was bringing us all to Europe, and their awards committee had selected me as an honoree. Now, Trish and I were on our way to a luxurious dinner on the Mediterranean coast.

Trish is more than my sister—she is one of my closest friends. I was thrilled to share this experience with her. As the plane thundered through the darkening sky, we truly did enjoy the fine food, comfy reclining seats, and fantastic service of first class. Our cabin made for an idyllic setting, and I should have felt relaxed. I was, literally, on top of the world.

But I wasn't relaxed. Something was bothering me.

SKY-HIGH NERVES

Anyone who works with me will tell you I am a supremely confident woman. I am a successful founder and CEO. More than two thousand employees work in my organization over a span of over twenty countries. We process more than two million W-2s each year, and we did billions in revenue last year. I have given hundreds of speeches, and I routinely meet with other CEOs and entrepreneurs. I have even counseled three presidents of the United States.

Yet I was nervous about this awards dinner.

During the flight to Monaco, I examined the list and read

the bios of the other forty-nine honorees. These were international superstars. Some were billionaire CEOs. Many ran global brands; they were household names. They graced the covers of *Forbes*, *Fortune*, *Inc.*, and *Fast Company*. One woman was the head of a global liquor and spirits empire; another was instrumental in Australia's most famous pearl dynasty. These women were celebrities of the business world.

But I was just...well, I was just *me*. A neighborhood kid from Tarboro, North Carolina, who grew up in the segregated South. While I had fought racism, sexism, and a lot of other "isms" to succeed in business, I didn't feel like anyone who belonged at an event like this one. I hadn't even ridden in a car until I was fourteen years old, never mind flying first class to Monaco. I was worried. *We've got a lot of work to do for black women*, I thought, *if I'm the one they invited.*

"Oh my God, girl," I said to Trish, suddenly a little panicked. My palms were sweaty and my heart was beating fast. "How did we get here? What if they didn't really mean to invite us? What if it's a mistake?"

Trish could see I was only half joking. "Girl," she replied, "they're going to have a lot of explaining to do if they invited us over and we're not supposed to be here."

My sister's a funny and pragmatic woman, and she always

knows just what I need to hear. She looked into my eyes. "Well," she said, "the plane tickets worked, so that's a good sign."

That cracked both of us up. "We're gonna party hard," she continued, "and embarrass them if they try to send us away." By that time, we were making a scene, laughing so hard. We made a pact: no more worrying. We were really going to enjoy this experience.

I WAS NOT ACCUSTOMED TO STAR TREATMENT

After we deplaned and passed through customs, a wonderful team of people greeted us. They held signs with our names printed on them and whisked us to a chauffeured limousine that took us to our hotel. In our room, beautiful gifts awaited us. In fact, every evening when we returned to the hotel, we found fabulous new gifts and fresh flowers waiting for us.

"These people are gonna have me breaking my damn teeth," Trish said after opening one of the gift bags.

"What are you talking about?" I said, as I looked over and saw her rubbing natural pearls on her teeth to see if they were real. They were.

Our hosts really treated us like royalty. At that point in

my career, I was not accustomed to star treatment. I still worried that I didn't belong—that I wouldn't be accepted. "Jan, can't you get out of that mode?" Trish said, trying to lift me up. "This is you! Look at this card. That's your name on it, right? This is you! You deserve to be here. You've earned it."

TWO TURDS ON A PLATE

The big event was a fancy gala dinner at the Oceanographic Museum and Aquarium, made famous by French conservationist Jacques Cousteau. The museum was incredible, built in Baroque Revival architecture style and set high on a cliff overlooking the Mediterranean. Princess Caroline of Monaco greeted us as we arrived.

The dinner was a big deal, prepared by a five-star chef. Everyone around us was saying that the ratings for chefs only go up to *four* stars, so this chef must be all that and more. But Trish was concerned—and for good reason, as it turned out.

When the waiters brought out the first course, Trish leaned her nose near the plate. She was sniffing it. "What are you doing?" I hissed. "Stop that."

"I'm trying to smell this to see if it's really what it looks like it is."

It was allegedly some kind of fancy pâté, and I'm sure it cost a fortune.

"It looks like two turds on a plate," she whispered.

We roared with laughter. Everyone stared at us, but we couldn't stop laughing. That was the highlight of the meal. It went downhill from there. I forget how many courses they served, but between the two of us, we barely ate anything. The food was too fancy. And it wasn't filling.

"Girl, I couldn't eat any of that, and if I keep sitting up in here without eating something, I'll get drunk," Trish confided as the waiters topped off her drink.

"Trish," I said, "don't drink the champagne! Don't drink the champagne!"

PEASANT FOOD

After it was all over, we were still hungry. Luckily, we'd made friends with our driver, Joelle. "Where do you go to eat?" Trish asked him as we climbed into the car. He was supposed to take us back to the hotel, but Trish had other ideas. Joelle listed a bunch of fancy fine-dining restaurants. Trish called him out.

"*You're* not eating there, though. Where do *you* go to eat when you're hungry?"

Joelle tried to refuse Trish (not a good idea). "Oh no, Madame, you do not want to go to the restaurants that we go to."

"Yes, we do. Take us there."

Joelle hesitated, but we insisted. He made us promise we wouldn't tell anyone. Then he took us to a restaurant where the locals eat. He described it to us as a "French peasant restaurant."

It is one of the best meals I've eaten to this day.

Many years later, we still laugh about that experience: two turds on a plate prepared by a five-star chef, followed by a French peasant meal that was out-of-this-world delicious.

Maybe that's just who we were—two sisters from Tarboro. Invited to the big time and loving every minute of it.

Growing up, we all understood that we were expected to share—everything from clothes (not just as hand-me-downs, but as hand-me-yours for the day as well) to books to ideas and knowledge. Many nights in my home, it was common for the older siblings who excelled at one subject to serve as homework master to another who could use the help. And so it went with tasks and toys and even the latest dance steps. Sharing this experience with Trish was natural for me; it made all the sense in the world and really made this experience one of the best of my life. Besides, she too had earned it! She was my rock.

One of the many things I admire about Trish is that she embraces life and enjoys the full experience. In a way, I experienced and enjoyed that trip through her and by watching her embrace it. She broke it all down for me, and that's when I became comfortable in the joy of it.

WE'RE ALL THE SAME; WE JUST HAVE DIFFERENT JOBS

We met some incredible women on that trip. What struck me was that each, in her own way and to a different degree, felt the same emotions I felt. At cocktail parties, as the women sipped wine and champagne, they began to open up. They shared their feelings of worry and self-doubt. That was the moment it occurred to me that *everyone*—no matter how big a mogul or superstar they may be—comes with their own set of insecurities and vulnerabilities. I'd been so focused on mine that I didn't realize the other women were feeling the same way.

We were all women, entrepreneurs, and sisters in countless ways. It didn't matter where we came from; we were more alike than different. We shared basic needs. Every one of our hotel rooms had shampoo, mouthwash, and toilet paper. We're all human. We all used, and needed, them.

My husband, Bernie, tells about growing up in England. One day, the queen came to visit his small village of Rodley in Yorkshire. One of Bernie's young friends mentioned that his father's company custom-made toilet seats for the queen. "Toilet seats for the queen, mate?" he asked. "Well, if the queen needs a toilet seat, then she can't be that much different from us. She's just got a different job."

It's in that spirit that Bernie and I have raised our two children. And we've taught them that it works both ways. Other people aren't better than you, and you aren't better than other people. We've all just got different jobs.

That Monaco trip was a real eye-opener for me. On the flight from LAX to Monaco, I was feeling apprehensive and vulnerable. I wondered if I was worthy of being honored along with that impressive group of the world's top fifty female entrepreneurs. But by the time we flew home, I had a new outlook. I was running with the big dogs and holding my own. And I was so incredibly grateful that my sister, Trish, was there to support me and share that incredible journey. Some say it's not the finish but the journey that matters most in life. For me, it's not just the journey but the *sharing* of it all that makes the journey complete.

Introduction

Never Compromise Who You Are Personally to
Become Who You Wish to Be Professionally

I KNEW THEY HAD GUNS. BUT THAT DIDN'T DAMPEN the festive evening. After all, being armed was their job. In fact, they made me feel safe. Everyone was dressed in tuxedos and elegant ball gowns, even the Secret Service agents guarding the president. We were at the annual Congressional Black Caucus Gala, and the highlight was a chance to get a little face time with President Bill Clinton.

I had met President Clinton once before, a few years earlier at the White House. (In fact, I've been invited to the White House by Presidents George W. Bush, Bill Clinton, Barack Obama, and the Trump administration.

Each invitation was to participate in discussions about jobs and employment, particularly women and minority job creation.) Nevertheless, I was a bit anxious during that meeting. I was also confident. When we came face-to-face, President Clinton was warm and friendly with charm to spare. Each time I met him, I was struck by his extraordinary ability to make each person he was talking with feel as though they were the only person in the world, the only person who mattered. It was a gift, and he had perfected it. But I also felt he was genuinely interested in people, which is a great quality for a president.

His behavior never wavered. Even at the Congressional Black Caucus Gala, when he was surrounded by hundreds of elegantly dressed dignitaries and their spouses, and he was shadowed by Secret Service, President Clinton made each person feel special. And that included me.

THE MOST IMPORTANT PERSON IN THE ROOM

In our company, we have a saying, a mantra, that President Clinton embodies perfectly. We ask our employees, "Who is the most important person in the room?" The correct answer isn't "The most powerful person in the room." It's not "The biggest client in the room." It's not your boss nor the CEO. We teach our employees that the most important person in the room is the person with whom they're speaking right now.

I've learned a lot from my interactions with presidents at the White House, not the least of which is the importance of integrity and the effect it has on you and on the people around you. For example, President Clinton made a promise to help flood victims in the small, historic, and 96.5 percent black town of Princeville, North Carolina, immediately after Hurricane Floyd devastated that community. Every home and structure in Princeville was under water after the storm. It encountered this fate after a decision was made to open the dam that protected the state capital of Raleigh from more severe damage. Princeville hugged the historic town of Tarboro, where I grew up. In the aftermath of Hurricane Floyd, many families lost their homes and worldly goods. President Clinton looked me in the eye and told me he'd help make sure anybody who had owned a home before the flood could again own a home if they chose to. And he was true to his word. However he is measured in history as a president or as a world leader or husband, I know he kept his promise to me and the hundreds of black families who needed his help. Since then, I have held him in high esteem for that huge moment of integrity.

INTEGRITY MATTERS

One of the central themes of this book is that in business and in life, integrity matters. In fact, it's so fundamental that having it—or not having it—can define a person's entire life. History and business are full of case studies about people and companies that either had no integrity or lost it somewhere along the way. Bernie Madoff. Enron. Arthur Andersen. Lance Armstrong. Bre-X. Volkswagen. WorldCom. Martha Stewart. The list is endless.

None of my family members, nor I, should ever end up on that list. Growing up, no matter what we were doing, we would ask ourselves, "Would we be okay if Daddy could see us now?" That was our checkpoint. Our integrity dial.

In business, you will be constantly tested. Your morals, values, and ethics will be challenged time and again. To ensure that your integrity remains intact, you will have to check yourself often. If I'm faced with a decision where ethics are involved, I simply remember to ask myself, "Would I be okay if Daddy could see me now?" Then I instantly know the right thing to do.

The title of this introduction is a motto that I live by. It's another value we teach our employees. Never compromise who you are personally to become who you wish to be professionally. Because if you do, any gains you make will be tainted by the fact that you diminished yourself by turning your back on what you know is right. In the coming chapters, we'll explore this subject deeper in the context of career and business.

WHAT THIS BOOK IS

I started my business, a personnel and staffing company called Act-1, in 1978. As an African American woman, I believe I had to overcome more challenges than a white man might have had to. My company began small, with a tiny office in the back of a rug shop in Beverly Hills. I decided on that location because it afforded me accessibility to service both highly skilled office workers and the companies that hired them. For many years, we were a small, local company. Then we grew into a regional company. Eventually, we made the leap to national, and then to international. Today, the ActOne Group is a multi-billion-dollar enterprise, with four distinct divisions providing forward-thinking talent, resource management solutions, and technologies to companies across the globe. We operate in over twenty countries and have over three thousand full-time employees.

Growing a company from a one-room office into a multinational conglomerate is unusual, but it's not unique. Doing it as a female African American is getting closer to unique. And doing it in the staffing, employment, and human resources industry—well, I'm going to go ahead and call that unique. But let's not get caught up worrying about labels.

The point is that my journey has given me keen insight, valuable experience, and extensive knowledge about a wide range of topics relating to entrepreneurship, business, careers, success, family, values, leadership, race, gender, empowerment, hard work, risk, and even germs in hotel rooms. Along with many other topics.

When I speak at events and conferences, no matter where they are in the world, I am asked the same questions over and over. *Should I start my own business? How do I become an entrepreneur? What's the recipe for success? How do I find a mentor? How do I discover my own personal brand?* And many others. I'll address all of these questions and much more in this book.

A WINDOW INTO GLOBAL BUSINESS

My unique experience is fueled and informed by my window into a wide range of enterprise organizations, working at the very heart of what feeds their success—the talented people they hire. I have a front-row seat because we are providing the talent. My company isn't just providing people, we provide skillsets.

Similar to the way a physician gets a good look when she gives a patient an examination, I see the inner workings of countless organizations. If I'm providing a certain skillset to a Silicon Valley company or to a large manufacturer in India, I get a window into how that company operates. I can see how they recruit, compensate, retain, and value talent. I see how they spend money. I know what skills and experience are sought within which industries. With nearly forty years in the field, I have seen the trends in hiring and firing, and I've been through more economic ups and downs than I can remember. I've learned to spot what works in business and entrepreneurship, and what doesn't.

What I'm going to share in this book is what is commonly referred to as "the secret sauce"—the core principles and values that have driven my success as an entrepreneur, a parent, a wife, a daughter, a sister, a friend, and a human being. It is what has driven the success of countless enterprise clients. Disclosure: The sauce really isn't a secret. The way to achieve success is no more a mystery than how to lose weight. But like losing weight, it's not easy, so people keep looking for new or different approaches. I've come to believe that there is no formula for success, but there are ingredients to success. We'll talk about those ingredients in the coming chapters. Just as the ingredients are important to success, so are the instructions on how to put it all together. Knowing when to act, when not to act, and how to act work together as a necessary formula. Understanding that an appetite for risk is essential, modulating your actions matters. It matters a lot. Along with cooperation, calculated spontaneity is essential. What some might call "acting up." Stepping out of the expected or normal behavior to achieve a goal by your own predetermined actions that don't follow the rules.

WHAT THIS BOOK IS NOT

Whether you're an employee, an entrepreneur, or an aspiring entrepreneur, and whether you're black or white, male or female, this book will share with you the lessons I've learned. I'll show you how I did it, how you can do it, what to look out for, and how to maximize the gifts and talents you already have. But I don't consider this to be a self-help book. You'll learn many valuable lessons along the way, but the purpose of the book is to share the insights and revelations I've uncovered during my life's journey. It is my deepest hope that you'll be educated, inspired, energized, and encouraged to pursue your best life and career.

As a woman, I can identify with and speak to the struggles of women in the workforce. And I will, in the coming pages. But this is not a book just for *female* entrepreneurs. Many young women ask me questions like, "What advice would you give *a woman* who wants to start a business?"

Or "What advice would you give *to a woman* who wants to recruit and hire the best talent?" "What advice would you give to *a woman* who isn't happy in her job?" My answer is always, "The same advice I would give to a man." The principles of success do not depend on gender, even if the techniques differ and the biases exist; they work equally well for all.

Women do face certain challenges in the workplace that men typically do not. We'll discuss some of these in the coming pages. But the overall ingredients for success are the same for everyone. What works for men will work for women and vice versa. How to work it is the thing!

Similarly, even though I am black and can speak volumes about the challenges faced by minorities in business, this book does not focus on that. This book is for *all* entrepreneurs of every color—whether you work for yourself, for a startup, or as an employee in a big company. You don't have to own your own business to be an entrepreneur. We'll discuss this concept in detail in the next chapter.

DON'T SKIP THE SIDEBAR ELEMENTS

Throughout the book, you will see three different types of sidebars. One is titled "Mama Says." My mother has been instrumental and essential to my success. She taught my siblings and me some of life's most important lessons, and she continues to live her belief system. She walks the talk, as they say. What she talks about is wide, smart, and soul-provoking.

She is an incredible role model, and I live my life every day by many of her sayings and beliefs. Growing up, we used to call them Mommy-isms. It's funny because, in my company, people refer to some of the things I say as Janice-isms, but most of those sayings are actually Mommy-isms. So look for the "Mama Says" sidebars and enjoy them for the down-home, Southern maternal wisdom they contain. In fact, I feel one coming on right now.

MAMA SAYS
ALWAYS BE YOUR BEST SELF

As kids, Mama used to tell us, "You should always be your best self when you're alone, and then you don't ever have to worry about how to behave when you're in the presence of others." This is a dose of pure and delicate, yet powerful, Southern etiquette that can build character in any child or adult. Mama said this applies whether you live in a low-income, high-income, or no-income household. She was right every time.

The second sidebar type comes from my wise and wonderful husband of thirty-four years, Bernie. He is the most positive person I have ever met. Anything can go wrong, and he'll say, "You have to be positive about it. You can't live in fear." That's one of his big principles: you can't live in fear.

My husband has taught me so much and was supportive from the first day we met. He is hands down one of the best business teachers I've ever had in my life, and he likes to say that I have been one of his best influences. It's not an overstatement when I say that Bernie is my hero. When Bernie introduced me to the book *The Art of War* by Sun Tzu, he taught me how to apply its principles to business. *The Art of War* is central to a lot of what we teach in my company. Throughout this book, you'll see sidebars titled "The Art of Bernie," which will draw modern-day business lessons from this classic book that dates back to the fifth century BC.

THE ART OF BERNIE
TASKS AND RESPONSIBILITIES

After reading *The Art of War* over a hundred times, I consider myself a devout student. The fact that ActOne Group reached the mark of a billion-dollar company without going public is a tremendous accomplishment, and we owe a measure of our success to Sun Tzu's brilliant work. It made it abundantly clear that to be invincible, everybody has to understand their tasks and responsibilities.

This principle is essential in hiring. If the result is not satisfactory, the manager will have to take responsibility. This means improving who they hire, evaluating their training, and if necessary, changing the employee's title and role. They must fill the position with someone who can meet the conditions set forth in order to ensure the team is successful. Teams who succeed in this regard will be handsomely rewarded and recognized.

—BERNIE

The third sidebar type includes short quotations or sections of text that warrant highlighting. These might be quotations from famous business leaders, from my family members, or from me. If they're from me, we call them "Janicisms."

JANICISMS
NOBODY IS SELF-MADE

I don't believe anyone is self-made. No one can do it all by themselves. Anyone who has achieved anything did it with the help and guidance of others. We are all ants on the shoulders of giants.

Altogether, these three types of sidebars will add different perspectives and emphasize key points throughout the book.

Before we tackle some of the best lessons of life and entrepreneurship, let's make sure you clearly understand my meaning for entrepreneurship. We're all familiar with the traditional definition, but after forty years of running my own company, I've come to see it as much broader than just starting and owning a business. Let's explore this in Chapter 1.

Part One

The
Foundation

CHAPTER ONE

◇

What Is Entrepreneurship?

MY CHILDHOOD WAS FILLED WITH ABUNDANCE. Although my parents had eleven children, we never wanted for anything. I can't remember a time when we lacked a hot meal, clothes, or supplies for school. Our dinner table always had cloth napkins, not paper. We frequently had guests over for dinner, and we gave things away to our less fortunate neighbors. Now, I didn't ride in a car until I was fourteen years old. But then, almost everyone we knew walked most places in our small town, as there was no public transportation. There was a taxi service, but taking a taxi was considered extravagant or special in those days, so we walked. Walking wasn't a fitness thing we did, it was normal for everyone, young and old. As a child, I didn't think it was strange at all. In fact, when I was growing up, I was convinced we were well-off.

That is, until I went away to college. That's when I realized we were actually, technically, poor.

Let me rephrase that: I realized we didn't have money. The United States government, statistically, considered us poor. My siblings and I felt like we were well-off because my parents were very efficient. My mom never threw away anything, and that's a large part of why we never lacked anything. "One man's trash is another man's treasure," she used to say. For example, the reason we had nice napkins at the dinner table is that we would cut and stitch cloth napkins out of old, worn out sheets. We used to make ice cream out of snow because the snow was free *and clean* back in those days.

ENTREPRENEURSHIP RUNS IN MY FAMILY

I was raised around entrepreneurs. My mom's family was entrepreneurial. Back then, her parents owned a barbecue restaurant. Not the kind of barbecue you see today covered in goop and sauce. Real North Carolina vinegar and chopped barbecue.

At the time, Tarboro, North Carolina, was a racially segregated town. There was the black side and the white side.

And there were two or three Jewish families, as I recall. Panola Street was the divide.

The white folks came to the black side of town just to eat at my grandparents' barbecue business. The whole restaurant was run out of their home. The dining room was set off from the rest of the house, and it had a door that opened to the outside. My grandpa built steps up to the door so that it looked like a proper restaurant entrance. My mother's entire family would help with everything, from cooking and chopping the hogs to folding napkins to helping with the whole operation. Even today, my mother can recall the names of firemen and other whites who regularly ate at Grandma Dora and Grand Daddy Dan's restaurant. She tells humbly of how her parents had a simple system of measurement for the black clientele (back then called colored) who came to buy barbecue lunches or dinners from the back door. They were considered "foot clientele," which meant they lived in the neighborhood, walked to pick up their meals, and took them home to their tables as neighbors. The number of mouths to feed in the family determined the amount to be put into the takeaway bags. Simple. One price fits all— their twist on one size fits all.

Grandma Dora and Grand Daddy Dan owned land, lots of it. Some of the land was farmland in rural North Carolina, and some was in our town. They kept a vegetable garden in the backyard of their home in Tarboro and raised chickens inside coops and turkeys outside that walked on raised metal nets. Dora and Dan were entrepreneurs, and the business disciplines they taught our mother as a child were passed on to us when she and Daddy raised our family. Our home truly was a business, as hers had been. Dad was the CEO and Mom was the COO.

My Aunt Sarah was also quite an entrepreneur. She was our paternal grandmother figure, as she raised my father from an infant after his mother, her sister, died during childbirth. Sarah was a schoolteacher, but she saved her money and invested in real estate. She owned several homes in our neighborhood that she rented out for additional income. You could say it runs in my family. It's in my blood. I was destined to be an entrepreneur one day. You might also notice that *female* entrepreneurship is in my blood!

Although my grandmother leading families and businesses was close at hand for me, the most important gift in life I've ever received, hands down, is that my parents were such excellent role models. Most of what I do in business I learned at home. My mom was a dynamic example of who and how I wanted to be in life. At that time, I thought she was just a terrific mom. I didn't really appreciate that she was also an excellent manager and leader until later in my life. I learned so much from her. I like to say that mine is the business my mother built.

THE DEFINITION OF ENTREPRENEURSHIP

The dictionary definition of an entrepreneur is "a person who organizes and operates a business or businesses, taking on greater than normal financial risks in order to do so." Basically, that definition says that only a person who starts a business is an entrepreneur. I disagree. Entrepreneurship encompasses much more than that.

But I understand where that limited definition comes from. With the greed-fueled craze surrounding startups and venture capital and IPOs and overnight billionaires who are still in their twenties, it's easy to see why the news media exalts that definition. Startups are sexy. Owning your own business is exciting. Fortunes are being made by brilliant tech company founders. I get it and I celebrate it.

But my definition of the word "entrepreneur" is much broader than that. I firmly believe *anyone* can be an entrepreneur, even if they work for a big corporation. You might call that being an *in*trapreneur. This is an important part of entrepreneurship that is not glamorized by the media.

NO MATTER WHO SIGNS YOUR CHECK, YOU WRITE IT

I believe that no matter who signs your check, you write it. In other words, you are responsible for your own income, whether you are the founder of your own startup or an employee of an established company. If you work for someone else, you can still be an entrepreneur by getting new clients, bringing in new business, generating revenue, and creating shareholder value.

Let's say you're a staff accountant for a CPA firm. If you see your job as an entrepreneurial opportunity, you go out and bring in new clients, and work hard to build and grow with your organization, watch how fast you get promoted and your paycheck increases as your portfolio grows. On the other hand, if you see your job as a necessary evil, and you put in only the bare minimum effort without any consideration for the success of the firm, your pay will stagnate. I guarantee it. No matter who signs your check, you write it.

JANICISMS
BLACK-OWNED BUSINESSES

I never thought about starting a black-owned business. I thought about starting *my* own business. I've always known I am Black, even with the iterative changes in racial reference I've lived through. I was born colored, then in my adolescence became Negro, followed by teen years—under the influence of musician James Brown—many of "us" debated back and forth before becoming Black ("Say it loud. I'm Black and I'm proud!"). By the time I reached adulthood, we "evolved" to being African American, and these days rotate between being Black or African American. The interesting thing is, when I was colored, that was always a lower-case designation. Once I became Negro, upper-case letters were used to define me. Interesting?

This concept applies to almost everyone who is on a career path. No matter where you sit on the corporate ladder, you can think and act like an entrepreneur. If you just graduated from college, this especially applies to you. If you're a mid-level manager, you can accelerate your career by acting like an entrepreneur. If you're a senior-level executive, you probably already know that what I'm saying is true.

OUR EMPLOYEES WRITE THEIR OWN CHECKS

In my organization, we believe in fostering an entrepreneurial mindset, and we're blessed that the type of work we're engaged in easily allows us to do this. If you look at how our company is structured, entrepreneurship exists at every level of the organization. Each employee budgets and plans for their growth. That employee is part of an office that collectively plans under a manager. That manager is part of an area that must collectively meet its plan. That area is part of a region, and so on. Our higher-level executives have more than one region that reports to them. At every level, the people who succeed and make

---

JANICISMS
ENTREPRENEURS WITHOUT PASSION

An entrepreneur without passion is just a person with an idea waiting around to see if it will happen.

---

a lot of money are the ones who look at their piece of business as an entrepreneurial venture.

And we reward those employees who take on an entrepreneurial spirit through our Founders' Club. Every February, we take our top performers on a peer vacation. In 2016 we took five hundred people to Jamaica. They got an all-expenses-paid trip, we wined and dined them, and we celebrated them. They got to network, meet other executives, celebrate with colleagues, and be praised in front of their team and significant others.

Many of our employees have greater compensation, more authority, more flexibility in their work and in their budgets, and broader opportunities than most startup CEO founders ever will. For example, one of our executives manages a piece of business that's worth $700 million annually. In fact, most of our top executives handle business that is far larger than most entrepreneurs' businesses. These people are vital. They participate in ways that are defined by their initiative, and they're focused on outcomes. They build teams who perform at such peak levels that they become highly valuable to the organization. So the organization works hard to keep them happy, rewarded, and well cared for. For them, I have gratitude and great respect.

In contrast to the perks and benefits of being an *intra*preneur, most entrepreneurs who start companies are under tremendous pressure to survive, let alone succeed. They have to answer to investors and shareholders. And most CEO founders literally have everything they own riding on the success of their companies. They are under intense pressure to deliver results. Of course, if the startup succeeds, then the rewards can be exponential.

So I don't believe the common definition of "entrepreneur" only applies to startups and business owners. I believe anyone has the right and ability to be an entrepreneur within any organization.

THE ART OF BERNIE
EMBRACE WHAT OTHERS WON'T

A long time ago Bernie told me, "Lovey, the biggest difference between people who achieve what they want in life and people who don't, is that the people who achieve what they want in life embrace the things that people who don't achieve resent." With my own eyes, I have witnessed this time and again, so I know it to be true. If you want to succeed, you must do what most other people are unwilling or unable to do. Embrace hard work. Embrace getting up early. Embrace risk. Embrace clarity. The more you embrace the things other people won't, the faster you will succeed, and the father you'll go.

SUCCESS IS TRANSFERABLE

We hire entrepreneurially minded people every day. When someone has all the ingredients for success, that's a great start. But they must *execute* those gifts and put in the time and effort to succeed. Once you combine the ingredients for success with the right work ethic, you can succeed on multiple platforms and in diverse industries.

I like to say that success is transferable. Remember,
through my company, we've hired thousands and thousands of people. This has taught me that success is an
expertise. It's like being a CPA or an engineer with a specialty, except the specialty is success. When someone
has proven they can succeed in one industry, I believe
they can switch careers to a totally different industry
and succeed there as well. Excellence is transferable.
You don't need to look as much at a candidate's level of
experience in your industry as you do at their experience
with success.

As employers, we tend to measure an employee's success
by the balance sheet and income statement. But to that
employee, success is very personal. Some of the same
things that have made men and women successful in
business make them feel like failures in their personal
lives. I have a friend who was the president of a multinational company and, by all measurements in business,
was very successful. But he felt his personal life was a

complete failure. He grew apart from his wife, as she'd not kept pace with the growth of his career journey, and when he earned a ripe early retirement, he felt thrown back in time versus moving forward in life. When it comes to success, you must measure what matters to you.

WHAT YOU ASK SPEAKS VOLUMES ABOUT YOU

Whenever I interview someone for a position in my organization, it's a pretty good indicator that they have a shot at being hired into the company. So when I'm meeting with them, I'm more interested in what they want to know. My interviews are often, therefore, a series of opportunities for them to ask me questions or to share with me what they're questioning in that moment, as opposed to me questioning them. Job candidates tend to focus too much on talking about themselves instead of asking the bold questions of the hiring organization.

In sales, if you don't ask that question, you may not learn some key data point that will inform your decision on whether or not to work for the company. You need to ask the questions boldly and quickly up front that save you the pain and process near the end of a relationship. Unless you're asking those questions that matter to you, you're not going to get the information that fully enables you to deliver the best product or service to that client.

JANICISMS
BUILD CONFIDENCE

The challenge I see for many of the women I talk with comes from within them, not from outward circumstances. But their challenge is not a lack of skill, capacity, or experience; it is that they lack confidence. Confidence is so important in business and career advancement. You can't rush experience; it will come in time. You can start building your knowledge now, but knowing your worth has to occur from the inside. Perhaps part of women's struggles is that they measure themselves differently and, in the process, devalue the rich competence inherent in their very nature.

There are always ways to ask a question that feels difficult. Don't simply trust what you see on the internet. Ask the question directly. Being bold about asking the questions that help you service the company better will pay off. What you learn will help you better understand what's required of you and what's expected of you by your client.

You owe it to your employees, you owe it to your customers, and you owe it to yourself to ask the questions, no matter how difficult they may be, no matter how big they may be, and no matter how entangled they are or how long it may take for you to get the answers. Ask the right questions, then listen, listen, listen for the right answers.

From the standpoint of the person doing the hiring, there are no magic formulas to looking for which is the better question for someone to ask you. If I'm in the position of interviewing someone, what matters to me is that they're asking questions that are relevant to the opportunity they're seeking and that dig a little bit deeper than the surface of who we are. More likely, they're asking about how we do things rather than what we do. My own perspective is that they should know what we do by the time they get to me, and if they ask that question, they've not been well vetted.

The other thing that's really important if you're in the position of being asked a question is that you encourage the person to feel safe to ask anything. Sometimes people will not ask the real question nor the big question that's on their mind because they may see it as a violation of protocol or etiquette. It becomes important for you to let the person know all questions are safe for them to ask.

If you are a business owner, or you are the business leader in the situation, and you're interacting with a potential client or current client, make sure that you reverse that and you let them know you would like to ask some pretty bold and frank questions. All of your questions should be aligned around offering better service. When you're interested in a company's best outcome, they're going to be much more open to giving you the honest answers you need to ensure that occurs.

The best way to get to know people is to ask questions and then listen. When you do this in business, companies will know how smart you are, how invested in their best interests you are, and how capable you are by the questions you ask, not just by the answers you give.

In meetings, one of the things that gets under my skin the most is when someone repeats what someone else has just said for emphasis, and then says, "I agree."

"Bob just said we need to look for ways to grow that account, I agree."

That's wasted time and wasted energy. My personal protocol is if you don't speak up, you are in agreement.

Inclusion and diversity of thought is something I encourage in the meetings that I run. So those people who are going to impress me, who I'm going to think about long after that meeting is over or who I'm going to invite to the next meeting or opportunity, are going to be those people who actually added something to the discussion, not those people who simply dittoed something. If someone is offering something relevant, something that drives the business forward, or something that provokes us to question ourselves or our processes better, then they've added value to the meeting, and they've added value to the business. That's where innovation can occur. That's also where personal development as well as business development will happen.

DISCOVER YOUR OWN PERSONAL BRAND

It's very important for anyone who wants to be an entrepreneur or grow their career to understand the value of defining their own personal brand and how it is relevant to the company they work for. This applies whether you are running your own business or working for someone else.

When you understand your personal brand, you will make better career choices. Your brand goes beyond images and appearance. It's more than how you dress or style your hair. Your personal brand is what *defines* you, through all your different career moves. It's who you are. It's what you believe in.

There is a simple method to figure out your personal brand, but it requires some effort. You'll have to put some thought into it, take notes, and do some quality thinking on this process. First, ask yourself the following questions: What do you pay attention to the most? Where do you invest your free time? Doing what? What do you find yourself thinking about most of the time? Write down the answers to those questions.

Now think about your work life. Do you want to sit in an

office all day, or do you like being out and about? Do you like meeting with clients, or are you an introvert who's more comfortable in the back office? Do you want to wear a suit or dress in jeans and a Star Wars hoodie? These types of questions will help you gain a better understanding of yourself, your preferences, and what interests you.

The next step is to compare those answers to your goals. This will help you figure out who you aspire to be. For most companies, the slogan or tagline represents who they wish to be at their best. Reaching that high level every day is a challenge. Defining your personal brand is similar. It is critically important that you figure out that brand, then live by it. Use it to make big life decisions like employment choices, your career path, and whether to start your own company.

Many young people don't do this. They fail to understand their own brand. When we help guide young people in their careers, we often see them make mistakes. They choose the wrong company to work for, accept the wrong job, or make a total career switch midstream. Even though they may have built their own personal website, they are not often connecting it to much more than advertising themselves. Sometimes they're lured by a higher starting salary without ever considering their personal brand, their goals, the company's culture, how they will fit in with the other employees, or even something as practical as the distance of the commute.

This personal branding exercise is something everyone should do routinely. The more clearly and currently you can define your personal brand, the better decisions you will make for yourself. But in this process, make sure you are not limiting your personal brand only to the way others see you. That does not define you. Rather, you want to fully understand how you desire to express yourself, and how you want to feel about yourself. Ultimately, you want to first understand and then embrace your personal brand so you can begin to expand and grow it. Often, mature people believe they know themselves, but like some younger people, they don't believe *in* themselves.

Sometimes, people feel that their personal brand should be what's represented by somebody else's life. They are influenced by what they see in the media. "You know what," they say, "I'm going to be like that person who has her own reality TV show. I'm going to be Ellen, or Oprah, Steve, DL, or Jimmy." There's just one problem: that isn't you, and you aren't them!

When you see successful people, be inspired by their success and try to learn from it. That's great. But translate everything into who *you* are, then see if it still fits. I can fit into a pair of booty shorts really well. But that is not my look. Often, I've told younger women, "Just because you can get into it doesn't mean it fits." The same principle applies to careers. Just because you can get a job at that company doesn't mean their team is a fit for you or you're a fit for them.

YOUR BRAND AND YOUR BUSINESS

Today, there are people who walk up to me at conferences or at airports and say, "You're that lady from ActOne." They know my company, but they don't remember my name. That's a big change from the early years of my business when it was the other way around. People knew my *name,* but I was just wishing they'd remember my *company.* This happened so much that for a while during those early years, my business card had the name of my company printed in big bold letters, but you had to really look at the fine print to read my name.

When you're an entrepreneur, *you* define the brand during those hard years and long hours before the business takes off. So be very careful you're building something that you want. Because when you experience success, the brand begins to define you.

If you start a company, you will be building your brand as you build your business. As an entrepreneur, your brand begins to define who you are to others. Once your brand is big enough that it has penetrated people's consciousness, that brand defines *you.* When you hear the name Mark Zuckerberg, who do you think of? You may know nothing about him personally. All that comes to mind, of course, is Facebook.

People intuitively understand branding, whether they know it or not. There are young women who paint the bottoms of their shoes red so they can be identified with that premium brand, Louboutin. Or people buy a knock-off Channel purse (with two n's) instead of a Chanel purse and hope you won't notice. They *want* to be defined by the brand. Personal branding works the same way—you will be defined, one way or another.

The development of my own personal brand is an ongoing, iterative process. My mantra remains, "Never compromise who you are personally to become who you wish to be professionally." But my experiences, my challenges, and my opportunities continue to frame and evolve who I am. At my core, it is very important for me to keep my balance, emotionally and physically, as I continue to grow through life. And it can be this way for you.

YOUR BRAND ONLINE

Recently, I had a text conversation with my son Brett about some important business matters. He asked me a particularly sensitive question. I was about to text back the answer when I instinctively stopped myself. Instead of putting the comment in writing, I sent Brett this message: "Not for text. Let's talk later."

Perhaps you've heard a common saying among lawyers: "Never put anything in an email that you wouldn't want to be read in court." I tell my employees a version of that. I say, "Make sure you're okay with what you're saying being on the front page of *any well-read journal.*"

The lesson here is one that many young people just out of college and searching for their first job learn the hard way. And it's something that I talk with college kids about frequently. Since I'm in the human resources and talent recruitment business, I know how employers screen applicants before making a job offer. Most companies always check out an applicant's social media profile. *Always.* Companies know that they can't control what you do online *after* they've hired you. That's why most companies conduct a thorough social media check *before* making a job offer.

And they should. Because the profile and pictures and comments that you post online *are representative of who you say you are.* If you're showing off a video on Instagram of you doing a beer bong, that's who you are to your audience, even though to you it may only be a fun snippet. You're *that* guy. You're a party animal. Your social media presence helps communicate your brand to the world. If you're applying for a job at a microbrewery, it might go over fine. But if you're interviewing to work at the police department or city hall, not so much.

KEEP YOUR PERSONAL BRAND PRISTINE

My advice to students is as follows. First, never post anything on social media that you wouldn't say in front of your parents. Second, never write anything offensive or incendiary in a text or email. Third, sometime before you finish your sophomore year in college, you need to get over looking at yourself on social media and start thinking about how an *employer* will view your pics and posts.

On the other hand, if an employer can't find you online, they will think you don't exist. So it's good to have a social media and online presence, but it needs to be pointedly clean. No drunk pics of you at the frat party doing a keg stand. No pics of you or your friends passed out and covered in beer cups. And no live videos of you and your friends doing anything stupid or that you'll regret later.

A potential employer will look at your social media accounts for a couple of reasons. First, they want to see if there are any deal breakers. Hate speech and angry rants will probably be deal breakers for *every* employer. Party pics might be a red flag for some employers but not for

MAMA SAYS
PRETTY IS AS PRETTY DOES

As I've shared, there were six girls in the house when I was growing up. When we were getting ready for church, or to go out, or to a dance, there'd be hair flying, debates over who got to wear which dress, and six girls pushing to get in front of the mirror. We were fairly close in age, and most of us, given the close age differences, could share clothes. My father worked at a dye factory, so the Bryant girls were known for wearing brightly colored jeans. Yellow, pink, red. The fashion of the time! But the color was unimportant compared to the way the jeans fit. And they didn't fit right unless we had to lie down on the bed and pull with all our strength to get them on.

We'd spend all that time and effort to look pretty. Then, as we were walking out of the house, Mama would say the same thing: "Remember girls, pretty is as pretty does." We understood what she meant: you can spend hours and hours trying to look nice, but it's your *behavior* that really determines who you are and how you appear to others. It's neither the makeup nor yellow jeans.

Mama led us girls by example. I don't recall a single time our mom asked us to do something she wouldn't do or behave according to a rule she didn't also follow. Pretty is as pretty does. Other people will pay attention to your actions, not just how you look. This lesson applies as much in business as in social settings.

It's no secret that Bernie and I are a match made in heaven. Our moms were, in many ways, cut from the same cloth. It was his mother, fondly referred to as Grandma Lizzie, who told me something during my second visit that has stayed with me for more than forty years. We were discussing child rearing and she shared with me what she said was the best piece of advice she could offer on the subject. It was, "Your children pay more attention to what you do than what you say!" For me, that sage advice adapts to any area of life's relationships.

others. The truth is, you never know. So it's always best to be safe rather than sorry.

Second, employers are trying to see if what you do and how you portray yourself online aligns with what they do. What are their business practices, and how do you match up to them? Do your actions reflect their values? How will their brand be protected, enhanced, or harmed by who you say you are online? All these questions will be taken into account.

It's not just potential employers who will look at your online profile. Your *current* employer also will access this information if they're considering you for a promotion, or even a bonus. You know who else might search for you on social media? Banks, lenders, employees. Even clients. Sometimes, when clients or potential clients are reviewing vendors, they want to know exactly who will be servicing their account. If it's a conservative company, such as a law firm or a nonprofit, and you have posted pictures online of you smoking a hookah pipe, that could hurt you. You could lose the promotion or that account.

To this day, I am extremely protective of my online image. For example, if I'm at a social event and I'm holding a glass, I always set it down before someone starts taking pictures. I'm not going to show up on a blog or on Facebook appearing to hold alcohol in my hand. Although I'm not judgmental of it, I don't drink. That's my personal thing. It is also my belief that some of my clients may not appreciate seeing that. I do not want to lose any business because of something silly like a Facebook post from a backyard barbecue.

The best thing to do is to get in the habit of *thinking* this way. Think in advance about how you want to portray your personal brand. Avoid any situations that could detract from that brand. Most people are accustomed to editing their thoughts before verbalizing them. But the real trick is to edit your thought before you *think* it all the way through. Protecting your personal online brand is one of the easiest and smartest things anyone can do for their career.

It's also a key component of empowerment. That's what we're going to discuss next.

KEY WISDOM AND INSIGHTS

- The meaning of entrepreneurship is much broader than the definition you'll read in the dictionary. It goes far beyond just starting your own company.
- You can be entrepreneurial in practically any job, working for almost any company.
- No matter who signs your check, you write it. You can be entrepreneurial in any job at any company.

- Success is transferable. It's not just about what you've done; it's about having and executing an entrepreneurial spirit.
- Protect your online reputation and think before you post. Your brand and your job depend on the presence you portray to the world.

CHAPTER TWO

$$\diamond\!\!\!\diamond\!\!\!\diamond$$

The Power of Empowerment

THE RED-HOT COALS GLOWED, MAKING THE DAY-light dim. Orange-yellow flames licked at the bottom of the enormous black pot suspended over burning logs. The light from the fire made our shadows dance across the big backyard that was shared by our extended family's three houses.

We must have looked like a coven of diminutive witches gathered around that boiling cauldron. I remember watching the liquid inside bubble over and drip down onto the fire. We would grab the posser with both hands and swish around the contents of the black cast-iron kettle, which was bigger than we were.

But we weren't making a witch's brew with eye of newt and wing of bat. We were making soap. Sometimes we were doing the laundry. There were many uses for that huge cauldron, and at times, it became a de facto gathering spot for the women and girls in our extended family. We simply called it "the pot."

We had the process of making lye soap down to a science. An essential ingredient in all soap is fat. So we boiled pork or chicken lard in the cauldron, mixed it with box lye, and turned it into soap that we used to wash clothes, sometimes dishes, and if necessary, us! As children, we would make fun of our neighbors who used fish grease in their homemade soap. "We're all that because we use lard and they use fish grease...eww." Mama and Aunt Sarah would chastise us about teasing folks like that, but we still did it.

As times got better, our bathing soaps moved up to Cashmere Bouquet for the females and Dial for the males. Mama got a washing machine, and we moved on to using powdered flakes bought in a box and Clorox bleach for the white clothes. For me, though, nothing could replace the day-long process of listening to the women in my family telling tales of our family, friends, and neighbors, or sharing philosophies of life. Making soap and washing clothes in that big cast iron pot had been ritualistic, and I missed it.

AUNT SARAH

Growing up with a large extended family, compounded as we were, helped me learn some of my earliest lessons about power and empowerment. I recall being lectured about many specific subjects by my parents and other adults in my big family. My siblings and I absorbed it as we watched the folks in our neighborhood interact, in particular, my Aunt Sarah. Aunt Sarah fancied herself as the matriarch of the family. Many of my childhood memories are centered around her.

Our family and extended family lived in several houses at the intersection of Cofield Street and Edmondson Avenue in Tarboro. My earliest home was at 904 Cofield. We grew up in a Bible-based family and community, and Cofield and Edmondson formed a cross in more ways than one.

Aunt Sarah owned several properties in and around town, and in some ways, those properties functioned as the center of our existence. Sarah owned the first house we lived in. Sarah owned the house my cousins lived in. Sarah owned the house our neighbors on the corner lived in. And of course, Aunt Sarah's house was owned by Aunt Sarah. Everything in our small world seemed to be owned by Sarah. The large backyards of these homes came together, and that's where we made the soap, did our laundry, played, and socialized. My mother's family owned their land, barbecue business, and other properties, as well, but when I was a young child, we lived on land belonging to Daddy's surrogate mother, Aunt Sarah.

Owning all that property affected Aunt Sarah. She had power and she knew it. And we knew it. Even as a child, I paid attention to how everyone else paid attention to what Aunt Sarah said and did. "Aunt Sarah said so and so." "Aunt Sarah did such and such." "Ooh child, don't say that to Aunt Sarah, or she'll do such and such."

With so many adults paying attention to what Aunt Sarah had to say, I began paying attention too. From her, I learned early in life that women could be strong leaders of families and communities too. As a schoolteacher working in the county schools, Aunt Sarah would, from time to time, bring children to her richly furnished home and have me come over to tutor them. My treats for doing so would often be a few nickels; however, my mother would remind me that the reward should be in my doing good. She'd say, "God never gave anybody a talent intended not to be shared. Your talent is in the teaching, Janice Elretha, not just in the learning." Mama was always talking about gifts and talents from God, and she was not about to allow any of her children to waste any!

Whenever Mama was serious, she called us children by both of our given names. Eleven children, and we all had been given two surnames each. We would joke that she purposefully gave us each two names so that she could use her own special system: one name called meant all's well and fine, but both names called meant "Alert!"

Aunt Sara was like the grandmama of our little family kingdom that felt so vast to me as a child. We all just naturally had respect for her. My mother was my first role model for who I wished to become in life, and Aunt Sarah was my earliest memory of seeing a self-appointed, empowered woman. I knew that someday I would follow my mother's examples of service leadership, and I knew that someday I also wanted to feel empowered like Aunt Sarah.

WHAT IS EMPOWERMENT?

There are two different dictionary meanings of the word "empowerment" that readily come into play here. The first is a straight, literal definition. It comes from the combination of the Latin prefix *em*, which means "to enter into or to become," and the root word "power," which means "the ability to do something or influence the behavior of others." Together, they form the first definition of empowerment, which is power given to a person in order to do something.

But it's the second definition of empowerment that most resonates with me. English is a living language, and words take on new meanings and different connotations over time. In our modern society, the word "empowerment" has come to mean the state of becoming stronger and more confident, particularly when it comes to being in control of one's life and one's rights. This is the definition that I'm referring to in the title of this chapter and throughout this book.

Empowerment is not just a cool word. It's a concept that I fought hard to achieve in my early career, and I still have to fight for it. Now it's something I strive to encourage others to fight for, for themselves—whether they're employees in my company or entrepreneurs or college students just starting their careers.

> **MAMA SAYS**
> WASTE NOT AND YOU'LL
> WANT FOR NAUGHT
>
> This was Mama's spin on the old saying, "Waste not, want not." We lived it. Remember, we were eleven children, a mother and father, plus anyone visiting, plus pets, in one house, in the South, on one income, with a garden to supplement our grocery bill. So we conserved wherever we could. To this day, all the Bryants are very frugal. For example, if we used a paper towel to dry our hands in my sister Sandy's house, even as adults, she would make us hang it up to dry so we could use it again to wipe a spill. And maybe a second and a third time too. She would always laugh and add, "Don't do that with the toilet paper, though." Guess you could say she was environmentally conscious early on.

THE ELEMENTS OF EMPOWERMENT

In business and in life, people who feel empowered will achieve better results and greater success. In their excellent book *The Progress Principle*, authors Teresa Amabile and Steven Kramer conducted research by analyzing nearly twelve thousand diary entries from hundreds of professionals. Their conclusion was that people are happier and more successful when they feel empowered and are making progress toward important goals. Had they asked me, I could have saved them the research!

Four key elements of empowerment are clearly defined goals, meaningfulness, support, and independence. First, the element of clearly defined goals. For employees to feel empowered, they need to know precisely what they're expected to contribute. It's not enough to ask a sales team to "increase sales." That's too vague. A clearly defined goal with a specific reward is required: "If your sales team reaches 150 percent of your budget this year, you will all be invited to the Founders' Club trip to Jamaica." When managers are empowered, their role becomes less about overseeing the troops and more about being accountable for specific results.

The second element of empowerment is meaningfulness. If employees are tasked with goals or objectives that they think are petty or meaningless, they will not feel empowered. They may feel that their talents are being squandered on low-level tasks that aren't important to the organization. In contrast, employees who feel their work contributes to the company's bottom line and overall mission will feel empowered and will want to contribute directly to the organization's success. This is especially true for millennials and younger.

The third element of empowerment is support. When people feel they are part of a supportive team working toward the same goal, as opposed to working alone toward an individual goal, they are more successful. Support also involves providing employees with the resources they need to reach their goals. Resources could include, for example, sales training, product brochures and information, software, access to relevant market data, industry intelligence, and so on. One additional element of support involves removing any barriers to success. If a team is continually running into the same obstacle, it's management's job to figure out a way to remove that roadblock.

The fourth and perhaps most important element of empowerment is independence. People operate best when they have a clearly defined and meaningful goal, a process, and support—and then the ability to work independently to reach that goal. Management that trusts their team members to accomplish their work and achieve their objectives however they choose is essential to empowerment.

THE ART OF BERNIE
LEADERSHIP

The Art of War makes it quite clear that if you wish to outsmart your competitors or be number one, you must have a tightly run ship where every member of the crew is totally committed to the ambitions of the captain and knows precisely what is expected of them. Every organization has a leader whose responsibilities are to focus on what needs to be done, maintain efficiency, and ensure that everyone clearly understands their part.

When the leader gives a command, it must be completely understood and acted upon by the responsible parties. If the plans of the organization are not carried out, then the fault lies at the level *above* the person who failed. To correct the situation, the leader must ensure that each member on board shares and supports the mission. This is vital not only to winning the battle but also to enjoying total victory.

—BERNIE

Managers should never micromanage; they should help eliminate obstacles but then get out of the way and let employees do their thing. When employees succeed on their own in reaching their assigned goals, it increases their sense of self-reliance, self-confidence, and autonomy. Then they are ready to take on even bigger goals.

It's not that different from understanding the empowerment we offer our children and ourselves when we allow them to exercise independence. Early on, our daughter, Kay, announced one day that she would like her father and me to leave home for a week and let her take care of her brother and herself. She was only five years old, but she was a very quick learner and she adored her brother. She always referred to him as "my Brett," and he enjoyed it for a very long time.

While we had no intention of honoring Kay's request to be left "in charge" for a week at so young an age, I have no doubt that she and her brother would have survived, maybe even thrived. Still, there are laws about such things. My husband says, "Rules are made for the guidance of babies and fools." Kay and Brett were no fools, but they were babies. My babies! I did begin to ask Kay's advice more on matters she knew were important, and I slowly began to set objectives for her and Brett that allowed them much more decision-making responsibilities and freedoms than most parents might. I believe it was the right decision then, and I continue to value their advice on everything.

As employees witness you making it your first priority to set clarity in place—clarity from which they can gain meaningful objectives and be supported by you—they will value the independence you offer and will reward you for it. These are simple, if not always easy, guideposts from which to measure progression. Everybody wins.

STAND ON YOUR F.E.E.T.

All entrepreneurs and most good employees thrive on empowerment. The feeling of having control over your own life and results can be a powerful motivator. Once people experience self-rule and autonomy, they are willing to work hard and reach their goals in order to maintain it.

In our company, we have codified this belief for our employees. We set basic guidelines for empowerment and, if employees follow these guidelines and meet their specific goals, they can pretty well do as they wish, so long as it's legal and honors others' rights. We like to say that our principle foundation is the F.E.E.T. we stand on. The F stands for the *freedom to innovate*. The E stands for *excellence in delivery*. The second E stands for *everything matters*. And the T stands for *time invested to understand*.

Our employees live by their F.E.E.T. They can win bonuses for achieving their specific targets. We would never tell our employees that something matters and then not have a data-driven metric attached to it that involves compensation. Everyone in our company understands that, and they pay close attention to make sure they hit those metrics to drive maximum compensation.

INFORMATION IS POWER

In business, one way to empower people is through information and data. My parents always taught us that information is power, and we teach all our employees we are in the information-gathering business. That's one of the first lessons new employees learn. Always, I say, if you're not a data-driven organization, you're not an organization.

"If you're not a data-driven organization, you're not an organization."

For example, we train our salespeople to stay away from adjectives in sales presentations. We stress that using data is more powerful. Don't say, "Most of our customers who started using our software saw tremendous gains in efficiency and productivity." Instead, say, "On average, our customers who started using our software saw a 32.5 percent increase in efficiency and an overall increase of 22.8 percent in employee productivity." You can see the difference in power between those two statements.

At the end of the day, businesses need data to make critical decisions. They need hard numbers. Which is why information is power, and it's a key element in empowerment.

INFORMATION AND ENTREPRENEURSHIP

One of the challenges for most entrepreneurs is that they tend to be driven by passion instead of data. Having tremendous drive and passion for an idea is a must for an entrepreneur. Without passion, few startups would ever get off the ground. But sometimes that passion takes the front seat and data takes the back seat. Passion without data leads to blind spots, and blind spots can sink a new company.

The same rule applies to gut instincts. Entrepreneurs are often successful in the early days just by following their gut. That works for a while. Maybe they score some big wins when they follow their gut. But if they rely only on their instincts when the data is telling a different story, that spells trouble. When in doubt, always side with the data.

I am also a firm believer in having intelligent timelines, which are another type of data. When you collect data and set goals, be sure to give those numbers a set timeline with hard dates for what you're going to achieve. Then you have to stick to those timelines, checking in on the progress of your goals regularly to make sure you're on track and moving forward at an appropriate pace. If you are missing your timelines, especially if you're missing them consistently, then you either need to readjust, course correct, set different goals, or maybe even stop and pursue something else entirely. Intelligent timelines that are well managed can assure that you meet your numbers and your goals consistently year upon year.

DATA VS. INFORMATION

Data and information are both important to a business. But there's a big difference between them. Data is the beginning stage of information. Data is a bunch of numbers, while information is the product of analyzing and interpreting the data. Data is inert; information is actionable.

JANICISMS
OWN STOCK IN YOUR COMPETITORS

I own stock in all my publicly held competitors. I didn't buy enough stock to have a voice. I just wanted to have visibility into the company, its financials, its data, and its strategy.

For example, a manufacturing facility produces loads of data that can be collected. This data might include the number of units manufactured per hour, cost per unit, inventory on hand, cost of raw materials, number of employees, productivity per employee per hour, number of line stoppages, cost per minute of line stoppage, and so on. Without analyzing those numbers, it's just a boring spreadsheet. But when an engineer analyzes and interprets that data, it may reveal that human error in the supply line is causing a lag in efficiency that could be solved with a new inventory software system. That's information. That's actionable. After all, the root word of information is *inform*.

"Give me six hours to chop down a tree and I will spend the first four sharpening the axe."

—ABRAHAM LINCOLN

CYBERSECURITY IS ESSENTIAL

No matter what type of data your company collects or

what size business you're in, it's essential to make that data as secure as possible from a cyberattack. Whether it's just you, or it's you and fifty employees, there are certain things that you have to be doing to make sure you protect your business and your clients from hackers. In 2017 one of my key clients was not the target of a cyberattack but became collateral damage to it. Due to the fact that we had cyber safety protocols set up, both physical and in terms of our actions, we were able to save that client a lot of grief in a way that other suppliers were not able to.

As I always say, no matter what size your business is, you are a global business if you're on a computer because you are accessible from anywhere in the world. You've got to recognize that and take security seriously.

One of the simple security steps that I think often gets overlooked by smaller businesses or individuals inside of an organization is a simple failure to lock computers. How many times do you walk away from your computer during the day, or at the end of a workday, and you don't lock it?

You must be very thoughtful about that if you're working in an environment where you're not going to be in front of your computer all the time. People can often see your screen. When sitting on an airplane next to someone, I can often see everything that they're doing on their laptop. Of course, I have no intention of harming them, but if they look over at my computer, they're going to see that I have one of those lenses on it so no one can see my screen from a side angle.

Conferences are a great place to learn about an industry, and when I go to one, I'm an excellent note taker. At a conference a while back, I was sitting there taking notes, and a man came up to me. He leaned over my shoulder and said, "Janice."

"Yes," I responded.

He asked me if he could have my notes.

"Excuse me," I replied.

He said, "I noticed that you were taking such meticulous notes. You've practically typed word for word what was being said. Would you share your notes with me?"

The fact that he admitted he'd been reading over my shoulder did not compliment me as much as I think he thought it did. My response was, "I've also put personal notes to myself in here, if you've noticed, so I will not share them with you. But thank you for the compliment."

Later, he even emailed me asking again for those notes.

The incident taught me that people can and will see your device screens if you let them. My daughter had long ago warned me that since I use a much larger print than some people, I was being easily read, but I didn't take it too seriously until that man actually asked for my notes because he'd been reading them.

Business leaders also need to be aware of phishing and spoofing emails. It's part of everyone's job not to let information unwittingly be shared outside the company. Many small businesses have all of their information, including their financials and bank accounts, residing on their computer systems, so they've got to make sure that they know how to avoid phishing and spoofing scams.

My policy on unsolicited emails is, "When in doubt, throw it out." Don't give credence to it. Never respond. Use password protection on all company email accounts and databases. Sometimes we get comfortable with our favorite password, and we don't want to change it, but it's a smart idea to change passwords regularly. It's really smart to make sure that your company has cyber protocols in place. These protocols are going to be required if you do business with certain companies or with the government. Even if you're a sole proprietor or solo freelancer, cybersecurity should never be ignored or taken for granted. Always be vigilant.

THE IMPORTANCE OF PREPARATION

Just as data and information can empower someone, so can preparation. Doing the prep work is essential, no matter what you're trying to accomplish, because it will empower you to do your best work. Being passionate and ambitious is a good start, but it's not enough. You must prepare.

For example, let's say you worked for three months trying to get a meeting with a prospective large client. They finally agree to meet with you. You would be a fool to go into that meeting without preparing, researching, rehearsing, studying the data, discerning information, creating your pitch deck, and knowing exactly what you're going to say and what outcome you're expecting to achieve. In business, a lack of preparation isn't just foolish, it's inexcusable.

Just the same, lack of preparation is a common mistake I see made by many of the entrepreneurs I meet. They get a great idea, then they jump in with both feet and start a business. But they fail to do the necessary steps before deciding whether starting this business is the right move at the right time.

"An unprepared entrepreneur is not an empowered entrepreneur."

An unprepared entrepreneur is not an empowered entrepreneur. At the very least, they should get proper business training, gain experience in the industry, do market research on the product or service they intend to offer, research the competition, estimate the size of the market, recruit and build a team, and develop a plan to finance the business. There are hundreds of books on these topics, so I won't go into detail on the steps here. But I will offer some recommendations for your reading list.

Another important element of preparation is self-knowledge. Once you have a clear understanding of the steps involved in starting a business, you should do an honest self-assessment of your skills, strengths, and weaknesses. For example, if you've never been involved in a startup before or built a successful company, that's a weakness that you can overcome with preparation.

Building a business from nothing is a unique experience with unique stresses and pressures that don't exist in other jobs. If you've never been through it before, prepare by either joining a startup or recruiting a startup veteran to join your team. At the very least, find an entrepreneur mentor who can coach you as you go through the process.

It's smart to get experience in the industry where you're launching your startup. But you also need general business experience. Being good at what you do, or having a

RECOMMENDED HOW-TO BOOKS FOR FIRST-TIME ENTREPRENEURS

Lean In: Women, Work, and the Will to Lead by Sheryl Sandberg and Nell Scovell

The Confidence Code: The Science and Art of Self-Assurance—What Women Should Know by Katty Kay and Claire Shipman

Thrive: The Third Metric to Redefining Success and Creating a Life of Well-Being, Wisdom, and Wonder by Arianna Huffington

The Road to Redemption by Lucinda Cross

Shark Tales: How I Turned $1,000 into a Billion Dollar Business by Barbara Corcoran and Bruce Littlefield

Good to Great: Why Some Companies Make the Leap...and Others Don't by Jim C. Collins

So Good They Can't Ignore You: Why Skills Trump Passion in the Quest for Work You Love by Cal Newport

The Art of the Start: The Time-Tested, Battle-Hardened Guide for Anyone Starting Anything by Guy Kawasaki

The $100 Startup: Reinvent the Way You Make a Living, Do What You Love, and Create a New Future by Chris Guillebeau

Rework by Jason Fried and David Heinemeier Hansson

The Founder's Dilemmas: Anticipating and Avoiding the Pitfalls That Can Sink a Startup by Noam Wasserman

The Lean Startup: How Today's Entrepreneurs Use Continuous Innovation to Create Radically Successful Businesses by Eric Ries

The Business Start-Up Kit: A Step-by-Step Legal Guide by Steven D. Strauss

The Art of Work—How to Make Work, Work for You! by Janice Bryant Howroyd

great product, is very different from being good at *business*. Business is an art in and of itself.

For example, you may be a gifted product designer with years of design experience who came up with a brilliant new kitchen gadget. But that design experience doesn't mean you understand sales, marketing, distribution, manufacturing, accounting, inventory management, capital structure, finance, and so on. Many businesses that fail don't fail because the product is bad, they fail because the management team lacks general business skills and experience. If the art of business is not your strong suit, build a team of people who have that experience.

ONCE YOU'RE IN, YOU'RE IN

There's one more key element of preparation if you aspire to be an entrepreneur. Before you jump in, it's very important to understand *why* you want to start a business. You have to *find your why*. There are many good reasons to start a business. A few bad ones too. But your reasons will be the foundation upon which your business is built.

Why you're going into business will determine countless details of your future company from the legal business structure you choose to whether or not you take on investors to how you build and grow your company. It's also important to realize that your reasons may change over time. That's fine, but even then, you should really understand the *why* at any given point in your journey as an entrepreneur.

It's important to understand your *why* because when it comes to starting a business, *once you're in, you're in.* When you launch a company, you have a tremendous amount riding on it. Your reputation. Your money. Your career. Your employees' careers. Your health. And a dozen other things. Once other people are depending on you and your company to succeed, you're committed for the long term. You can't just up and quit. The stakes are too high. So you have to do everything you can to improve your odds of success. In this, as in so many things, preparation is one of the most important things you can do.

MAMA SAYS
EXPERIENCE

Mama was a big believer that you can learn something from everyone, even if it's only what *not* to do. One of her favorite sayings is, "It's good to learn from experience. But it's great to learn from *someone else's* experience." So again, I recommend you read *Good to Great* by Jim Collins. It was recommended by a customer who highly valued the innovativeness we offered his organization. He became a mentor and a friend, and I learned a lot from him, and he credits his knowledge as enhanced by what he learned from this book.

MY MOBILE PHONE RULE

One type of unpreparedness has become a pet peeve of mine. We hire many millennials across my companies, and I've had the great pleasure of working with some wonderfully talented young professionals. After working with so many people in their twenties, I now have a rule: I insist that everyone fully charge their mobile phone before they leave home.

There are quite a few young adults in my extended family, and when I go back east to visit them, I am shocked at how often they leave the house with only 20 percent charge in their phone's battery. I tell them, "You don't have the luxury of leaving home without a charged phone. That phone may end up being your best friend."

This is especially true for women. Women should not be traveling through airports or jumping in Ubers, Lyfts, or taxis, or going to meetings with a 20 percent charge on their phone. First, if your phone dies, no one can reach you. It's rude to your clients, your coworkers, your boss, and your family. But also, that phone could save your life or the life of someone else if there's an emergency. It's just common sense in the world we live in to make sure the most important communication device you own has a full battery when you walk out the door. It's also a good idea to bring a charger with you. Anything less, I would consider a lack of preparation.

TEN STEPS TO STARTING A BUSINESS

Based on the US Small Business Administration Steps Listed at SBA.gov, but Updated and Revised by the Author

Step 1: Write a business plan, using business assistance and training

Step 2: Finance your business

Step 3: Determine the legal structure of your business

Step 4: Understand employer responsibilities

Step 5: Find local assistance

Step 6: Register a business name

Step 7: Choose a business location; even if it's a cottage startup, it needs a legal address

Step 8: Obtain business licenses and permits

Step 9: Understand the state, regional, and local taxes everywhere you plan to do business

Step 10: Register for all applicable taxes

More information at SBA.gov

READINESS IS AN EQUATION

Readiness is an equation. It's not just a point that you reach in life after a lot of preparation. It's actually formulaic when you're at your best. By that, I mean you start to apply the principles that you know which areas of growth and which areas of receding effort you need to give to get to where you want to be. So if you think about it, evaluating when you're ready for that next step is what it's all about. Whether that step is adding another employee or going after a new piece of business, it's going to require you to think fully about several areas.

Now those areas can include, but are not necessarily limited to, the following. First, what your ability is to scale. For instance, going after a piece of business may require you to be at one place at the beginning and another place in six months or a year. You know your business better than anyone else. You know what's in the pipeline. But you also know what's on the line. And having a real critical attention to the difference allows you to be ready.

So let's say you have good branding and an unbelievable offering and you go after a new client opportunity. The client may be impressed and may be ready to sign a contract. But are you ready to fulfill the order? You are the one who's behind the scenes, and you've got to make sure that you are ready in terms of scalability. You have to be able to deliver on what you promised. If you're not, that new piece of business could actually pose a risk to your current business. What's it going to cost you to deliver the new business?

Some people go after an opportunity, and they are able to gain it on a relationship basis. People trust that because of what you've done in the past, you can do more in the future. And you may gain that contract. But unless you're really thinking about all the areas of where you are right now—and do they add up to you being where you need to be for that new piece of business?—you can get into real trouble.

Or you can get into a really great opportunity. You're the one who has to make that call. Dealing with big companies often means different payment schedules than with smaller businesses. In other words, you may not get paid for a while. So you've also got to consider how long you can sustain delivery before you're paid for it.

It's the formula today for many enterprise-size companies, especially those who do business in more than one country at one time with any given supplier, to push out payments to ninety days and beyond. So you may be very well suited to deliver the business, but you can't sustain the payment terms. That means you may have to negotiate better terms in the contract. If you have an experienced salesperson or sales team, chances are they're negotiating these points before the business is even sold and before the client has even bought from you.

You've got to be very careful, very thoughtful, not to make the mistake that so many businesses do in allowing salespeople to be enthusiastic around bringing in opportunities in a way that allows them to appear to be negotiating on behalf of the company. An example of this is something that happens in many companies, where the salesperson is asked, "Can you do this? Can you do this?" And the answer may very well be yes, but then, when the conversation goes into, "And can you do it by this date, and you know we get it from this XYZ supplier for this amount. Are you going to be able to match that?"

Those are not sales questions. Those are negotiation questions. Now there are people in your organization who likely are answering these questions in some written format. But oral contracts are perceived to be a big part of your ethical performance. Negotiations should not be long in the first part of the sales process. Now when is this not true? When you're talking about smaller opportunity, it can be the case that you're going to handle it all in one conversation and a handshake. It feels great to do business on a handshake, but it's oftentimes not smart to.

So if we think about reading readiness clearly, the R is about resources. You've got to be resourced appropriately to the opportunity. Nothing can take the place of having in place what's necessary to do the business and fulfill the order. These resources are not just your ability to sustain payment terms. It also includes whether you have the product available. Or if you're selling a service, do you have the time available or the people available to give the type of service that you're going after?

The E is about education, but more importantly in businesses, it's about everything mattering. Everything matters from the beginning to the end, as my husband loves to say, from A to Z. So you've got the make sure that you're paying attention to what's being asked, what's being committed, what's being required—all the pieces of the equation that make business right.

The A is about authority. Who has the authority to sign contracts and make promises to customers? There are going to be levels of authority in any business and you should be very clear about setting yours up from day one, even if you're the sole employee of your business.

As a business grows, different people are going to participate in different ways. In many smaller businesses, sometimes people without important titles play key roles in decision-making. You've got to be clear about who has what authority in your organization. You can get into a lot of opportunity–and into a lot of trouble–if you're not clear with your employees about where the authority really lies.

The D in *ready* is about delivery. Everything you promise is worth nothing until it's delivered. Now when I say that, if you've got a great reputation, your reputation is built on what? The way you've delivered in the past, not the way you've promised in the past. Let's be clear: there are many review websites available to displeased customers and employees, so you've got to make sure that your delivery is spot on. You're going to have some disgruntled comments on social media from time to time as you build your business and your reputation, and most folks can see it for what it is, but nothing can destroy great delivery.

If you're out there doing what you say you'll do when you say you'll do it, how you say you'll do it, it's always going to defeat any negative press. The important thing is to focus on delivery.

So that's my definition of readiness. You've got to be well resourced. You've got to make sure that you understand the importance of education and that everything matters. Understand and clearly articulate who has authority in your organization. And always focus on delivering for the customer.

Readiness applies to anyone who's building a business. It applies to anyone who's building a brand. Because when you're interfacing with people and you're exchanging money or value for that, it becomes really important that you're definite about what that offer is and what that agreement is. So readiness applies whether you are in your first business or whether you're in the last legs of a huge business that you're about to take public. Readiness still applies.

It's a good thing to work from a readiness principle from day one so that you don't have to get yourself ready for better opportunities later in your business. Apply this principle from the moment you start your business, and it'll certainly help you as you continue to grow, particularly when you're not the one who has your fingers on everything in your business. It enables you to make sure that you've grown it in a way that it can sustain future growth.

EMPOWERED WARRIORS

The business world can be rough. It can be unfair. It can even get ugly at times, and it can knock you down. Business is war. There are wolves on Wall Street. And there is no guarantee that good will triumph. That's why our organization studies the principles of *The Art of War* and applies them to business.

Especially during the difficult times, it's important to remember your *why* and to understand your reasons for going down whatever path you've chosen. If you've prepared yourself properly, if you've empowered yourself with data and information, and if your *why* is strong enough, you will maximize your chances of success, and you won't quit when times get tough.

JANICISMS
LIVE IN GRATITUDE

One of the gifts I believe I was given is the ability to live every day in gratitude. Every moment, I live in gratitude. I'm in gratitude now. As I write this book, I have deep gratitude that I might share at least one thing with at least one reader that will make a positive difference for you in this moment. That's how I live in gratitude. That's how important it is to me.

Although we must always be mindful of the lessons we've learned from the past, we cannot dwell on the past. Too many people get bogged down by obsessing over mistakes or poor choices they made years ago. That does not serve you now. Take the lesson, learn from it, vow not to make the same mistake again, then look to the future. Lamenting what could have been or what you should have done differently will not help you achieve your future goals. You can't put your foot on the gas pedal to go forward if you're looking out the rear window. Remember that the goalposts for success spell READY—resourced, execution, attitude of gratitude, delivery, and yourself, because it's up to *you*.

In Chapters 3 through 10 of this book, we'll give you the tools you need to move forward and be ready to "act up-ward" to become *empowered warriors* ready to take on the business world. You'll be able to go head-to-head with the sharks without becoming one of them.

KEY WISDOM AND INSIGHTS

- Empowerment is the process of becoming stronger and more confident, especially in controlling one's life and claiming one's rights.
- The four key elements of empowerment are clearly defined goals, meaningfulness, support, and independence.
- If you're not a data-driven organization, you're not an organization. Data collection and analysis are crucial to any business.
- An unprepared entrepreneur is not an empowered entrepreneur. Take the appropriate steps before you launch your business.
- Once you're in, you're in. So you have to understand *why* you want to start a business.

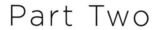

Part Two

Pillars of Entrepreneurship

CHAPTER THREE

◈

Education and Miseducation

MY SISTER SANDY PULLED UP TO THE TERMINAL IN a Doris Day-blue punch buggy. That's what I call it, anyway. It's also known as a punch bug, piggy punch, slug bug, punch dub, or punch car. But most people just call it a Volkswagen Beetle.

"Welcome to Los Angeles, Sister!" she greeted me.

Los Angeles International Airport (LAX) was very different in the late 1970s than it is now. It was busy, sure, but looking back, I think of it as quaint. You had time to say a proper hello or goodbye to your loved ones at the curb. Not like today, where security and airline associates manage daily security issues while serving often unhappy, weary travelers, and ground patrol shoos you away almost before you can put your luggage in the trunk.

I was so glad to see Sandy! I gave her a long sisterly hug. It had been a difficult time back home in Tarboro. My father had passed away a few weeks earlier, and Mama was devastated.

My father's death was sudden, unexpected, and tragic. He had taken two young men out fishing on the ocean and a storm came up. My father put the two young men in a life raft. But he didn't have one for himself. They didn't find his body for a long time after that. But I feel grateful, in a way, because my final memory of Dad was the sight of him hugging and kissing my mother goodbye. That was the last time I saw him alive.

My mother married my father very young, and she had never really lived without him. She spent two weeks in mourning, unable to get out of bed. When she finally got up, she pulled herself together and said she was ready to get back to living. I don't know if Mama ever felt truly whole again after my father died, but she's a strong woman, and I believe she battled her sadness and loss for many years afterward. She is my perfect example of someone acting up instead of acting out.

I had purchased my airline ticket to Los Angeles before

my father passed. When he died, I told Mama I was canceling the flight and staying with her in Tarboro. I knew she needed me.

But Mama wouldn't have it. She said that I needed a break, and she insisted I go enjoy time, as planned, with Sandy out west. I could tell Mama was beginning to bounce back, so I agreed to go. I had planned to come to LA on vacation, just to visit Sandy for a week or two. Little did I know I'd end up living that vacation for the rest of my life.

CALIFORNIA DREAMIN'

From LAX, we drove to the house in Ladera Heights that Sandy shared with her husband, Tom Noonan. It was my first time in California. I kept staring out the window at the palm trees. "Whoa, this is how you live out here?" I asked her. Sandy thought my wide-eyed awe was endearing and sweet.

Sandy and Tom's house was immaculate. I've been called meticulous because I keep my own home so clean. Well, Sandy was Miss Meticulous. She took cleanliness to another level. We got along great because neither one of us could stand dirt, and at that time, we both adored Carole King and Kim Carnes; they were at the top of our vinyl collection.

Because of Tom's career as a high-powered record company executive, Sandy was always entertaining and hosting parties for people in the music and entertainment industry. And mind you, Sandy's house was in Ladera Heights between Culver City, Inglewood, and Crenshaw. This wasn't exactly Beverly Hills. Nevertheless, singers and movie stars were always popping in to say hi. I was impressed.

A FISH OUT OF WATER

Sandy and her friends were sophisticated and gorgeous. They lived a glamorous lifestyle. My sister was also an incredible chef and loved to cook big, Southern-tinged, California-style meals for everyone. Some pretty big names would stop by just to eat her home cooking, which was famous. One day, I walked into the living room, and Gregory Hines was sleeping on the floor.

I felt literally like a fish out of water. Celebrities and musicians would come over and just lounge by the pool. But I had never learned to swim. My sister Zest, as a teenager, worked as a lifeguard and swimming instructor. She was like a fish *in* the water. Her hair always looked good, soaking wet or towel dried. Out of the six Bryant girls, I was the only one who had nappy hair. All my sisters had flowing hair. So I didn't want to go swimming, *ever*, and I never was motivated to learn.

So I didn't swim, and I didn't look or talk like any of Sandy and Tom's friends or the Hollywood types who were coming over. I didn't yet carry a purse with someone else's initials on it. I often felt like a country bumpkin in that glamorous crowd. My own sister looked more white than black, which made me feel even more out of place, even though I loved being *in* their place.

Sandy pulled me aside and reminded me that in Los Angeles, everybody is from someplace else and everyone talks differently. She said, "You're going to find that some of the best friends and the best people at the best parties all come from different places. So just go on and jump in the pool and the conversation, and feel good about yourself."

SHOULD I STAY OR SHOULD I GO?

Tom was a brusque Irishman from New York. He had a will of steel and a heart of gold. He loved my being there with them because Sandy was happier with me around. Sandy liked having family nearby, and she and I were best friends. Tom said he could see the difference in Sandy the day I arrived in LA. He would tell me all the time, "You mean so much to your sister. I've never seen a family like yours."

When I bought my ticket, I bought a roundtrip fare

because I planned to go back to North Carolina. After all, I only came to Los Angeles for a vacation and a visit. But Tom and Sandy changed my mind. I was really blessed that Tom was one of my greatest supporters. He said to me, "Don't go home to North Carolina. Stay in LA. Do it for yourself."

He insisted that I at least give myself a shot at life there. To this day, I tell people that I didn't decide to move to LA. Just as Tom had invented the "bullet" in ranking music to distinguish artists' trending expectations, he invented the decision and reason for me to stay out west. It turned into a golden opportunity for me to build a whole new life.

THE HOLLYWOOD STAR

One evening, as Sandy and I sat by her pool, I was flipping through a magazine. The article that caught my eye was about the world's most beautiful people. I stared at one of the pictures in particular. With dawning amazement, I realized that the list included an actor I had met.

"We met him!" I squealed to Sandy.

The weekend before, Sandy had taken me to a private event where we chatted with this individual. He was there as a guest, just like us. On the way home, Sandy and I had laughed about how he didn't look that great in person.

> **MAMA SAYS**
> ## IN ORDER TO BE OUTSTANDING, SOMETIMES YOU HAVE TO STAND OUT
>
> As a young girl, I was painfully shy and quiet. I didn't speak in groups unless I had to. So Mama would encourage me by saying, "In order to be outstanding, sometimes you have to stand out." I find this to be especially true in the business world, where I have to meet with clients, give presentations, and lead an organization.

He was just kind of ordinary. We joked about how disappointed one of our family members, who was a big fan, would be if they had seen him in his relaxed state.

Comparing this experience with his airbrushed image on magazine covers, and reading the adoring commentary about his physical beauty and success, I began to dissect what I thought I knew about the elements of fame. He wasn't particularly handsome in person. Without the team of people who earned a living making him look good, he was just sort of plain. Not only that, he wasn't a stimulating conversationalist. Without a script, he was boring. He was small in stature and big in ego. Yet somehow, he enjoyed a large fan base and a string of box office hits.

I found this puzzling. Luckily, as she had done on so many occasions, my smart sister provided some insight. She encouraged me to consider some things about the Hollywood star that would have been obvious to me had I not been blinded by his celebrity star power.

One thing she taught me that day stayed with me and has served me well over all these years in business and in life. She told me he lived his life based on how *he saw himself*, and then projected that outward, instead of seeing himself the way *other people saw him*. This actor had genuinely transformed himself into the person he wanted to be simply by *believing* he already *was* that person. Then it was just a matter of getting other people who held influence and positions of power to see him that way too. In order to achieve that, he had to *be* that person, not just *act* like that person.

I thought about this concept a lot. And I learned a couple of important life lessons. First, it taught me not to make judgments about people before I knew their story. Second, I realized that this principle doesn't just work for actors and entertainers. It can and does work for anyone who chooses to use it, no matter what career you are in. I began using this technique myself. It took a while, but eventually, it worked for me too. Still, I'm really glad that Cary Grant lived up to my every expectation when I finally met him. Gorgeous, elegant, attentive and silver-haired.

BANISHING NEGATIVE IMAGES

Meeting *that* movie star, and then reading the article about him that seemed so different from my experience, opened my eyes. Once I began to think through this whole idea of being who I wished to become, it became necessary for me to get rid of negative images of myself. One way I learned to do this was through writing affirmations.

In one of my favorite books, originally titled *As a Man Thinketh*, we are taught, "We think in secret, and it comes to pass, environment is but our looking glass." As a matter of fact, I love this little book—a pamphlet really—so much that I gained permission to edit and retitle it *As a Person Thinketh*. One more notch for women.

For several years, I recited two key affirmations every day, and they changed me in a dynamic and profound way. These affirmations are deeply personal to me, and I don't share them with anyone to this day. Even if I did share them with you, they would be of little help to you. Affirmations must be personal and specific to *you* and *your* life and goals.

In addition to writing affirmations, I began to rethink how I looked at myself. It was obvious to me that I was not going to change just by osmosis. I had to forgive myself for the negative thoughts I had harbored about my own speech, my appearance, and my worth.

It would be a challenge. The early images I had from looking at myself in the mirror, I measured against an impossible standard. I was a young black girl, but I compared myself to the media-based ideas of beauty—those images that we all saw daily on television, in magazines, and in movies. Those images in the media had not shown me any role models who were inspiring for me. I could count on one hand the number of black women on TV and in the movies, and still have fingers left over.

Although I had arrived in one of the most vibrant cities on earth, a place rich with opportunity, I felt ugly and out of place. I felt that there was no place for me in that city. But then my sister and that magazine showed me how one of the world's biggest stars had created his place and had taught people how to see him.

If he could do it, surely so could I.

My mother and father instilled in us Bryant girls the idea that life holds tremendous possibility. They were my role models. I wanted to emulate them in word and deed. They infused us with the belief that it was not just our right but our duty to do big things, especially in the service of others.

In Los Angeles, I was dipping my toe into a whole new world. My father had passed. My mother was 2,600 miles away. Thank God, then, for Sandy. She was helping me to explore just who I could become and how I could do it.

I may have felt out of place, but I knew if that diminutive actor could make others see him as the towering Adonis he saw himself to be, then why couldn't I become whoever I wanted to be? Years later, I received the gift of my little, aforementioned book *As a Man Thinketh*, which pushed this truth further.

LISTENING FOR THE LESSON IN A SEGREGATED SCHOOL

My hometown of Tarboro began as a Tar River settlement in the early 1700s and, with population growth, became the town of Tarborough (often misspelled as Tarrburg) in 1760. By 1763, Tarborough was the county seat for Edgecombe County. This had started out as a Tuscaroran land and was settled by Europeans, as so much of the East Coast was during that time period.

By 1831, Nat Turner's Rebellion caused white Tarboroans to fear the revolt of their slaves. (One hundred years later, in 1931, the plantation house for Oakland Plantation would be renamed the Elks Lodge and used by Blacks living in that portion of the town. It provided a center for community events in my childhood.) These citizens hated abolitionists and William Lloyd Garrison and his publication *The Liberator*. By 1860, there were sixty-four free blacks living in my hometown. Tarboro has its history of plantation life, and in my childhood, that history continued to reveal itself in subtle and unsubtle ways.

By the time I was in eleventh grade, the federal government had mandated school integration, but the town had not responded fully. White citizens were determined to ensure that predominantly black schools would not be integrated by white students; however, a few of us blacks would be allowed to attend the white high school. Out of pride, a handful of our smartest kids were enrolled to go. Guess who went? Years later, my girlfriend and I laughed—sober laughter—about who was smarter, the one who went or the one who held out. We still haven't answered the question.

Since I had never even touched a white person—not even in a handshake—until eleventh grade, going to an all-white school caused a lot of anxiety. Especially as a teenager, when I was in the middle of that difficult transition from self-consciousness to self-awareness. One day, the history teacher—a tall, thin, blond-haired, blue-eyed white man—began delivering a lesson on the topic of slavery. He stood up on the desk and described why blacks were so well suited to be slaves. Except he didn't call us blacks.

During that year, I often heard the N-word.

As he described his interpretation of the anatomy of slaves, I sat shaking in silence in a room full of white students. I didn't say anything, but my heart was in my throat. I bit down on the inside of my cheek so hard, just to keep from crying. I thought to myself, "Please Lord, don't let me cry in front of the class. Please just get me out of here, and I'll never come back."

I still have the scars in my mouth from where I bit down on my cheek. I may never be able to forget what happened that day.

I went home absolutely determined that I would *never* return to that school as long as I lived. But when I told my father what happened, he had a different reaction than I expected. He told me, "No one has the right to force you to decide how you feel about yourself. Only you determine how you feel about you. If it will make you feel better, I'll take off work tomorrow, and I'll walk into that classroom and tell your teacher exactly what I think of him. Or you can go back to school tomorrow, determined to get the best education possible, and you can listen for the lesson."

It took a moment for his words to sink in. If my father was willing to take a day off work, it was a big deal. That meant he'd lose a day's pay.

I also knew how important education was to my parents. They believed education was freedom. And I knew my dad was right. I had to put aside my personal hurt, my pain, my humiliation, and I had to be brave in the face of that mean-spirited environment. I had to listen for the lesson.

So I went back to the school, and I did as my father suggested. I was determined to learn everything I could in that school. For a long time after that, every evening when my father got home from work, he would ask me, "Janice, did you listen for the lesson? What was the lesson you heard today?"

Since then, no matter what is going on in my life, I try to listen for the lesson. This has helped me in business and every other area of life. I won't say I'm grateful that I attended that school, but I am grateful for the education and for the lessons I learned there.

To this day, I have a constant reminder of that challenging era of our country's history. Hanging on the wall in our corporate headquarters is a large framed picture of a little black schoolgirl in pigtails and bows. It commemorates the landmark 1954 US Supreme Court case *Brown v. Board of Education.*

MY REEDUCATION

Those years of growing up in the segregated South had deeply and surely suggested to me that I might, after all, be a little less acceptable to that big world out there. Living in Tarboro, I never saw anyone who looked like me doing the things I wanted to do professionally. Even my sister, who had made it in Los Angeles, didn't look like me. She looked white.

In a world that often values women based on dictated standards for physical appearance, I had negative images of myself—my looks, my speech, and my value. But here's what's interesting: not once did I ever doubt my ability to learn, do, achieve, and succeed. Thanks to Mom and Dad, I grew up believing I have everything I need to be everything I need to be. Whatever any job or career could require of me, I knew I could do it and do it well.

Sandy was my guardian angel in the big new world of Los Angeles. She taught me to respect all cultures and to smile whenever I was tempted to frown. She would tell me, "When you walk into a room, Jan-Jan, stop and take as long as you need to assess the environment and the people. Chances are the first person you notice who is smiling at you is the one you should break the ice with." I can't tell you how many times I've used this one technique alone.

Another one of her sayings was, "Switch up carrying things like your purse from hand to hand, and shoulder to shoulder throughout the day. It'll help you stay balanced mentally and physically." My all-time favorite Sandy-ism is, "Between your ears is the most valuable real estate you will ever own. Don't let people live there rent-free. If they're not contributing to the wholeness of where you want to be, then you need to throw them out."

Sandy taught me about the world in sound bites. She brought so much into my life by sharing with me the beauty of her own. She showed me possibility by helping me evict my own demons of insecurity.

It turned out that shedding a self-image that I had harbored for more than twenty years was not easy. It took courage. It took work. But I saw that it was possible, and that's what kept me going.

One by one, I began writing down things I didn't like about myself. Things I had spent years believing. I reframed them with respect to who, and how, I really am. Each night, I would write out my affirmations. I was determined not to let a single negative voice live in my head rent-free.

I would be remiss not to mention the importance of music

in my reeducation. Sandy and I would make a game of finding theme songs. Each negative image I struggled with required its own theme song. Thank you, Lionel Richie, Kim Carnes, Marvin Gaye, and John Lennon! Stevie Wonder, Johnny Mathis, Dolly Parton, James Brown, and Carole King. Thank you. You all helped me through my reeducation.

MY FIRST JOB IN LOS ANGELES

One day, Tom came home from work and told me that he and Sandy were leaving for a music industry conference in Italy and that he needed me to mind his office during his absence. I agreed. And that was my first job in LA—working for Tom.

He was the associate publisher of *Billboard Magazine* at the time, and he attended a lot of music conferences. So shortly after I was hired, Tom and Sandy went to Italy for that conference, and true to his word, he left me in charge of his office while he was gone. When he came back, I had made some changes.

There were dozens of aspiring musicians who worked at *Billboard* at that time. They worked their day job at the magazine just to pay the bills, but what they really wanted to do was write songs and perform music. Their heart really wasn't in the day job.

> **MAMA SAYS**
> ## IF GOD MADE IT, THERE MUST BE PERFECTION IN IT
>
> Mama didn't believe in putting people down, looking down on people, or feeling self-righteous or scornful. She believes that there is beauty in everyone, even if you have to look a little harder sometimes. "If God made it, there must be perfection in it."

So while Tom was gone, I fired several bad temps. And I hired their replacements. I wanted people working for Tom who were excited to be there, not people who were just going through the motions. When Tom came back, he was like, "What did you do?" But he soon realized it was a good thing and that I had a good eye for employee talent. I learned that I enjoyed finding and hiring the best people for the job.

And that is how I first got the idea to go into the staffing industry. When my temporary job at *Billboard* ended, I decided to go out on my own. I opened my very first office in the back of a rug shop in Beverly Hills. All I had was a tiny desk and a phone book. I struggled to get clients in the beginning, but I was determined to succeed. Just like the Hollywood star I told you about earlier in this chapter, I decided to *see myself* as a big success, *believe* I was a success, and then *become* that big success. And that's exactly what I did.

IF IT'S NOT WORKING, THROW IT OUT

The many lessons I gained from Sandy and Tom taught me that I had a lot more to learn. They helped me realize the importance of always learning, being curious, not judging, and soaking up as much knowledge as possible from as many experiences as I could.

But they also taught me that I had a lot to *unlearn*, as well. I have had to let go of many of the things I thought I knew about life and the world. I have battled through the comfort and discomfort necessary to win my success. I have learned to throw out anything that is not working or does not serve me, my company, my employees, or my family. This concept of unlearning will become very important as you follow your own entrepreneurial path.

In any career, you must be realistic and pragmatic, and be willing to see the world as it is. Recognize the way the world works. But then forge ahead with your own dreams and visions to create the world you want to live in. Work to become the person you want to be in that new world. In order to accomplish this, you need to learn about yourself and learn to love yourself—even if that means unlearning many of the things you've believed for most of your life.

KEY WISDOM AND INSIGHTS

- See yourself as you wish to be, then project that to the world. This principle works for anyone who chooses to use it, no matter what career they are in.
- It is not just your right but your duty to do big things. You have been given gifts. It's your obligation to use them.
- Use daily affirmations to change your own self-image.
- Don't let people live in your head rent-free. If they're not contributing to the wholeness of where you want to be, stop listening to them.
- If it's not working for you, throw it out. If you want something different in your life, make a plan and execute on it.
- Aim first, then shoot.

CHAPTER FOUR

Disruption without Interruption

HOLLYWOOD HAS CHANGED OVER THE YEARS THAT I've lived in Los Angeles, and lately, it's been changing dramatically. We've all watched as the entertainment industry has faced classical disruption.

First, the music recording industry faced massive disruption by peer-to-peer file sharing, Napster, iTunes, digital downloads, and the death of CDs. The Internet and digital technology were like a freight train slamming into the Capitol Records building. That industry will never be the same. My brother-in-law Tom was a recording industry executive, so he saw the disruption up close and from the inside, sharing much of what he saw with me.

As this book goes to press, movie and television studios are facing their own disruption. What was once singularly referred to as "the industry" and "the studio system" is now a global network of multinational, multimedia technology corporations operating from a cloud platform. Companies like Netflix, Hulu, and Amazon are dominating distribution and disrupting the traditional studio model. Technology and more informed customers have made an impact, not just in Hollywood but across all industries, blurring, merging, and redefining geographies and boundaries in a rapidly shrinking world.

GOING GLOBAL

Today, businesses can be *born* global on day one, versus slowly *growing* to become global over many years. That is the way it used to be done, and the way we did it at my company. If your business is on the Internet, your business is global, even if you don't think it is. That's very important because most businesses begin small. They think of themselves as only local or regional. But every business is local and every business is global. You're local because wherever you are at that moment delivering that service, you have to understand what is necessary to succeed in that local market.

You're global because of two things. First, your reach via the Internet becomes global. Countless entrepreneurs have set up their business and become a success overnight. My son has a friend who started a business, and his first customer was not in the United States.

The second reason you're global is because no matter where in the world you're located, no matter what you do, there's somebody else in the world who can do that too, and your customers have the option to use you or use them. Customers have access to them via that same Internet.

Customers are more aware and have more choices than ever before, and they communicate with each other constantly. Never mind those multi-million-dollar, feel-good ad campaigns—the Internet can make or break what were once-dominant blue-chip companies. So we need to understand that when we set up our businesses.

THE IDEAL OF DISRUPTION

Enterprises—large, medium, and small—are looking for ways to do more than just stay relevant. They are looking for ways to be *disruptive* and, by doing so, expand into new markets. But disruption is a difficult goal to achieve, and most efforts fall short. Let's examine what companies are striving for when they seek disruption, and then we'll look at what often actually happens in practice.

Almost every company today talks about disruption as

the way they'll create new markets or vastly expand into existing ones and, in the process, displace the established market leader. They talk a good game about disruption, but it seldom comes to pass. This is especially true with mature blue-chip corporations. In most cases, they're not disrupting anything.

Big established companies take forever to change or to launch new product categories. That's because their decision processes are designed primarily to eliminate risk. The desire to reduce risk ends up causing analysis paralysis. They get bogged down in endless product iteration and evolution run by committees. So instead of creating a market-changing *disruption*, their attempt becomes nothing more than an unhealthy *interruption*. Often, the product never gets to market at all.

It's okay to try to reduce risk. But you cannot eliminate it. The whole nature of business is taking risks. Without risk, there is no business. If a company is unwilling to take risk, they will not innovate, and they will never disrupt.

"The whole nature of business is taking risks. Without risk, there is no business."

Mature blue-chip corporations are just not nimble in the way that new businesses run by upstart entrepreneurs are. It's not just the age of the business that prevents or slows disruptive ability; it's the scale of the business. Large multinational enterprises have too many moving pieces, and since all these pieces have to be accountable, they don't move as quickly or as dynamically as they would like. Think of the largest organization on the planet, the US government. How long does it take to get something done? How much innovation is happening? How much waste occurs in the process of moving something forward? In 2016 the US presidential election results were an outcome of frustration and desire for disruption.

Entrepreneurs are not managing that type of scale or that many moving parts. We can be a lot more aggressive and a lot more dynamic in our risk-taking. The result is that entrepreneurs can often effect the disruption that they want to see in an industry. Meanwhile, the huge corporation is still doing product design and market research.

ACTUAL DISRUPTION

True disruption is when an innovation creates a new solution to service an existing market that is so much better than the existing solution that it displaces the companies currently serving that market. A classic example: when the advent of commercial air travel disrupted train travel. A more recent example: when digital photography essentially destroyed the photographic film industry. There are thousands of examples of industries that have been and are being classically disrupted.

My husband, Bernie, likes to tell his story of the iceman who delivered ice by horse and buggy to his mother's neighborhood in Lancashire, England, when she was a little girl. He says that the iceman was kind, and his ice was always clean. He would give children chips off of his ice blocks and tell them fun stories. He knew his customers by name, and his horse knew the neighborhoods by street. That horse would automatically stop without urging at each customer's front door. He served that community for years and witnessed marriages, births, and deaths. He paid attention to his customers, but he did not pay attention to his market. He thought he was in the ice business. He never recognized that his customers used ice but that they sought refrigeration. Until refrigerators became a household appliance.

The best time to try to disrupt is either before you start a company or in the early days of your company. Ideally, you find a gap in the market or find a mature market that has the potential for disruption. Then you innovate a new product to disrupt that market and build a company around that product. In other words, design your new company specifically and from day one to be a disruptor.

Unfortunately, human nature often works against that

ideal. Most entrepreneurs are conservative in the early days of their company. They only have a finite amount of cash on hand, and their burn rate is a specific amount per month, so they reduce risk in hopes of making the money last as long as possible. This is faulty thinking. The best and safest thing a startup can do is make progress toward disrupting a large market. If you can do that, there will be no shortage of investors willing to fund you. In fact, they'll beg you to take their money. This is a part of what I call "acting up."

There is a simple model for creating healthy disruption. It follows the five questions that journalists are taught to ask:

- Who: define who will be impacted, who will not be impacted, and who will be the drivers of disruption early on.
- What: define what the outcome targets need to be and what processes will be used to engage.
- When: set timelines and specify when key actions, results, and evaluations will occur.
- Where: clarify and arrange where disruption will likely hit and where it should have the greatest impact.
- How: establish how appropriate communication and measurements will occur across different metrics, units, and timelines.

JANICISMS
DOCUMENT PROCESSES

Whenever you figure out a new system, a better method of doing something, or an improved strategy that works, document the process. Write it down so you can share it with others in your company and so it can be replicated. Don't just write down the steps; also be sure to document exactly what you learned from the process.

If you memorialize the difficult things you're doing today, they become the easy list tomorrow. If you're not documenting, then you're really just working from the gut, and you'll lose some of the important lessons you could have passed on to make it easier for the next person. We are sticklers about documentation in our company.

Process documentation has been practiced in the medical profession for centuries. When doctors do surgeries, for example, they document the process. That way, what is considered an experimental surgery today becomes routine tomorrow. Many of today's routine surgeries are only routine because the pioneers of that surgery documented the process and what they learned while doing it.

HOW WE CAUSED DISRUPTION IN THE STAFFING INDUSTRY

It wasn't that long ago that companies seeking outsourced, managed solutions around workforce usage looked for different providers for different needs. They would choose one company to provide the technology and process, and a separate company to provide the actual staffing. The rationale was that a healthier, more robust effort would be given to finding and recruiting talent into their organizations if different companies staffed and managed the process.

This approach was inefficient. I saw the advantage of a single company that could provide both. So we went out and built it. In order to ensure excellent outcomes for our customers in this space, we designed Acceleration. It's a suite of workforce technologies that are customizable and scalable for companies in almost every industry.

This product has wide applications. It not only serves global enterprises that engage in mergers, acquisitions, and new product and service lines, it also serves midsized clients that need competitive analysis and other robust solutions that support their growth. In many ways, our Acceleration product disrupted the industry by bringing together two essential elements that previously had to be purchased separately.

Today's competitive business landscape highly values this type of innovation and disruption. Change in an industry can occur both from internal and external factors. Sometimes change occurs too fast, sometimes too slow. But knowing your change potential is important for any business, especially for entrepreneurs who are planning to disrupt entire markets.

NOTHING NEW IS BEING INVENTED

When it comes to disruption, companies do not need to recreate the wheel. Yet every startup or capital-funded venture company tries to say they have invented an entirely new product, a novel process, or a new way of doing something that will revolutionize and disrupt the XYZ industry. I don't buy it. Nothing truly new is being invented. All companies can do is grab something that's already there and reconfigure it toward a better use or a different outcome. In other words, they're putting a new spin on something that's been around for years.

For example, the process of paying someone to drive you somewhere in a car has been around for a hundred years. It's called a taxicab. Uber just put a new spin on that age-old model. Renting out a room in someone's house has been going on since the very first homes were built. Airbnb just modernized the process by using technology. They didn't come up with some incredible new product or mind-blowing invention.

Yet both of those companies, Uber and Airbnb, have disrupted entire markets. You don't have to be a supergenius coder or a rocket scientist with a new invention in order to disrupt. You just need to look with new eyes and a fresh perspective at what's already there, then reconfigure it. The most powerful tool for disruption is not a patent lawyer; it's your own imagination and ideas. Just think about the Internet and how disruptive it has been to many businesses, communities, and economies.

COMMON SENSE IS NOT THAT COMMON ANYMORE

When I began Act-1 Personnel Services, perhaps the biggest risk I took is one many entrepreneurs take out of necessity. I depended on my common sense more than on experience, knowledge, and research. I lacked formal business education, training, and experience as an entrepreneur. I had heaps of good old common sense, most of which I learned from my parents growing up. It's all I had.

While common sense is a gift to any entrepreneur or business, it is not that common. I have seen plenty of Ivy League–educated MBAs make foolish mistakes that defy logic. You may have amazing book smarts and intellect but still lack common sense.

I am blessed that in my early days as an entrepreneur, I achieved many desired outcomes and business opportunities by relying on that common sense. The bigger a business grows, the more likely common sense will fail to produce positive results. At some point in a company's growth, common sense must be augmented by data, information, research, analysis, risk assessment, building out a team, and optimization efforts. I could not have built the large organization I did without all of those things, and especially not without my team.

THE IMPORTANCE OF CLARITY

You can't bake a cake without the proper ingredients. In fact, if just one of the key ingredients is missing, like flour, for example, the end result will not be what you want. Success works much the same. There are certain essential ingredients that must be present in order to achieve the desired result. The obvious ingredients have been written about and discussed ad nauseam—hard work, for example. Everyone knows you have to work hard and put in the hours if you want to be successful. But I want to explain one of the lesser-known ingredients to success.

That essential ingredient is clarity. As in all aspects of life, the clearer something is, the more profound it is, the more valuable it is, and the better outcomes that can be predicted. Whether that is clear data and analysis of a situation, or whether that is simply the clarity on the bookkeeping and the accounts in the church and how you're going to fund the summer programs for kids. No matter where we look, clarity becomes important. It is especially important in your career in business. The truth is that very seldom will you find successful people who weren't clear on what they wanted to achieve. To reach a goal, you have to first clearly define it and what it looks like, then hold that clarity vividly in your mind as you work toward that goal.

The chances are that you are going to have a much greater chance of success, no matter what that success is determined to be, if you bring clarity not only to what you're going for but also clarity to the people who you're working with, who are important to your achieving it. Take Gandhi, for example. Gandhi became really clear during his career about what he thought would be important for India and the message it represented to the world. Because he was really clear on who his people were, he was really clear on what was going to be needed to create the type of success he was looking for. As a result, he was able to see change in his lifetime.

JANICISMS
ENTREPRENEURSHIP VS. LEADERSHIP

Leadership and entrepreneurship are different skills. But they are related. You can be a great leader but a lousy entrepreneur. But you can't be a great entrepreneur without also being a great leader.

Once you get in the habit of appreciating the value of clarity, you will develop the skill of getting clear in all areas of life. That is a huge benefit. Getting crystal clear at the beginning of whatever you start is the key to finishing the project successfully. Sometimes you're able to achieve even more than you expected when you are clear on what you want the outcome to be. So if you're going to invest your time and other people's time in something, make sure you're clear on what it is you're aiming for.

If you are an employer or a manager of people, one of the fastest ways to lose their engagement is to not have clarity. Clarity on the mission. Clarity on the purpose. Clarity on the communications and protocols. Employees perform best when you give them specific marching orders and a clear target.

You may have heard the old saying, "Shoot first, aim second." Too many people adopt that bad habit in their career. They think, "I'll just work really hard for a few years, and I'm sure I'll end up someplace good." Wrong! That strategy doesn't work. The only way to get where you want to go is by taking the time to deliberately and thoughtfully mapping it out. Always aim first, then shoot.

BEING A WOMAN ENTREPRENEUR IN A MAN'S WORLD

Being a woman entrepreneur today is a lot easier than it was in the 1970s when I started. And being a female entrepreneur in the United States is a walk in the park compared to what it's like in some countries around the world. I've traveled the world and seen with my own eyes the struggles that women business owners endure. I remember in India seeing a woman carrying a heavy load on her back, leading cows across the street, all with a baby strapped to her chest. I have great admiration for all women who have succeeded in business anywhere, especially in developing nations.

I've been blessed to experience and understand the sisterhood of women that exists around the world. It's a sisterhood that is needed, important, and can be helpful in sharing our stories. You don't have to live through something personally in order to benefit from it. You don't need to be a woman to believe in a woman.

Even though women have made tremendous progress in the four decades since I started my business, there is so much more to do. I often travel as much as three weeks out of a month. Many times, when I go into airport lounges or into a restroom on an airplane, I am reminded how much of the world is designed for men and not for women. Look around at some of the air lounges that have not been updated in any big airport and notice how many accommodations for women you see. Not many. Plenty for the guys, though. No acknowledgment that women are also road warriors. In many places and instances, service is designed for the business*men* but not for the business*women*. Long ago, experiencing antiquated design in airline restrooms, I realized that the world needs more girls and women in STEM studies and sectors. Thankfully, some airlines and aircraft builders are finally realizing this too.

"The world needs more women engineers and entrepreneurs to design our future."

Products and services that are designed *by* men usually end up being designed *for* men. I have found this to be the case in many instances and industries. In some more progressive companies and industries, these gender issues are improving. But as with all self-improvement, change happens in spurts and sputters, unless it's deliberately and strategically planned. Simply put, the world needs more women engineers and entrepreneurs to design our future.

WOMEN IN TECH

No part of our economy is untouched by technology. To exclude women from this important world is to exclude women from a large part of the economy and a large part of the wellness of the world. Women are a critical and important force in business because we bring a lot of value.

Data shows us that organizations led by women are more inclusive in searching for solutions and creating processes, so investing in women in technology would only provide more value. Women business owners hire a mix of genders and often diversities of race and ethnicities and generations. That means they get diversity of thought in their product. We women get things done. We know that women's lives are built on multitasking, and this leads to our ability to balance many projects at various stages of completion.

In my business, that's the truth. We focus on excellence. We don't let it go until it's done well, not simply done. Look at how many women businesses have overcome epic challenges to deliver excellent quality, not to mention big returns for investors. So I'm a huge proponent of venture capitalists looking at women differently.

KEY WISDOM AND INSIGHTS

- If a company is unwilling to take risk, they will not innovate, and they will never disrupt.
- The best time to disrupt is before you start a company.

Find a gap in the market, then innovate a new product to disrupt that market and build a company around that product.

- The most powerful tool for disruption is your imagination. You don't need patents or breakthrough technology to disrupt; you need creativity.
- A reliance on common sense must eventually be replaced by data, information, research, analysis, risk assessment, and optimization efforts.
- The world needs more women engineers and entrepreneurs.

CHAPTER FIVE

Keeping the Humanity in Human Resources

MY MOTHER USED TO TELL US BRYANT GIRLS, "Always behave as if what you do in the dark will come to light." That was before camera phones, before Instagram, before Facebook, before phones recorded video, and before security cameras were everywhere. These days, Mama's advice rings even more true because it's easier than ever to get caught on camera misbehaving. Her point was, if you're always on good behavior, you won't have anything to worry about.

Most human beings, I believe, operate from intuition and conscience. Intuition happens *before* you do something, and conscience is what you get *after* you've done it. If you think you're going to get away with something illegal or immoral just because nobody can see you, think again. Eventually, you'll be found out.

You can be in the ladies' room and think you're having a private conversation. Years ago, that was where we went to talk. I laugh when I hear men say, "Oh, ladies always go to the bathroom in pairs. They never go alone." Well, maybe we ain't going in there to pee! Today there's always somebody in the next stall with a cell phone who is ready to hit record if something juicy or incriminating is discussed.

Technology has brought light to some very private places, and it's smart to be mindful of that. Whether it's bad behavior, whether it's an intimate conversation, whether it's innocent, or whether it's mean-spirited, someone can record it, edit the footage any way they want, and blast it out to millions. Within minutes.

There aren't many places where people can behave poorly and not be found out sooner or later. We live in a world where you can't even go into a cave in the woods without the risk of getting busted. Even if you do find a cave, you still have to be wary of the echo!

TALK FROM YOUR STRENGTH

When we make presentations, my teams are encouraged

never to speak negatively about our competition—even though I know our competitors have made presentations where they've spoken negatively about us. I don't want anything negative like that to come back on my company. So I tell our teams, "Always talk from your strength. Even if you're asked about your competition, talk from your strength."

There are so many examples of people who ignore this rule, and most of them have paid the price. You may recall back in 2015 when high-level movie executives at Sony Studios watched helplessly while their hacked emails were made public. When they were writing those emails, they believed no one would ever see them. They were wrong. The embarrassing content of those emails ended up costing studio head Amy Pascal her million-dollar-a-year job. Pascal later said, "The content of my emails was insensitive and inappropriate but is not an accurate reflection of who I am." Many who know her agree.

That's a tough lesson to learn. It's always better to behave in line with your true character. You can pay a steep price simply because you momentarily stepped outside of who you are ethically to have a moment of fun. It's not worth it. Act as though the mic is always on.

It may seem obvious, but so many senior executives still don't get it. I once witnessed a major world figure nearly make this mistake. He was wearing a microphone and being videotaped at a conference. Then he said, "Will someone tell me when the video is no longer recording so I can tell a few jokes with the students." *Nooo!* Some of us had to remind him that the cameras are *never* off. If your jokes aren't suitable for grade-school children, you shouldn't be telling them to anyone. If you tell a juicy joke at a conference, you can bet it will be splashed across social media within the hour.

It doesn't pay to step outside of who you are for any reason at any time. Find your personal code of ethics and live by it. Always think twice before you step outside of your best self.

TO THINE OWN SELF BE TRUE

I was raised under the principle of that great quote from Shakespeare's *Hamlet*, inspired by Socrates, "To thine own self be true." I even like to expand that a little. I say, "To thine own self, and to others, be true." It is very important to self-check your inner communication. Is the voice of your conscience telling you that it's not comfortable with your actions? If so, you need to course correct.

Pay attention to that inner voice. You don't always have to accept it as absolute, but take it as an important data point in your decision process. It's equally important to check yourself on how and what you communicate out to others. Many lives have been harmed or ruined for failure to read, edit, and delete before pressing send! Just ask Amy Pascal.

A career in business will test your morals and ethics. Being true to yourself and your character is not always easy. But your authentic self should never be compromised, even if it means sacrificing easy wins. Violating ethics policies or even breaking the law may lead to short-term gain, but long term, there is nothing more important than your reputation. Our company's reputation for honesty and integrity has been key to our enduring success.

Another thing that keeps me in check is a close connection to my large family. Each of my siblings, as well as my Mama and my children, talk and visit regularly, no matter how busy life gets. My family members are a funny, bright, and socially aware bunch. Not much gets by them. They are the touchstone for everything we grew up believing and valuing. If my moral compass ever gets skewed, they'll let me know. They'll call me out. I appreciate that.

WOMEN FACE SPECIAL CHALLENGES

The challenges women face in the workplace include all the same challenges men face, plus more. Many of the processes and measurements of strength and performance in business are male-defined, so they can put women at a disadvantage.

Let's think about what happened during World War II. Many women stepped up magnificently on the home front to meet the special challenges and needs of a nation at war. Not just by keeping the home fires burning but by producing products for the war effort, managing their communities, and growing local economies.

The fictional character Rosie the Riveter became a cultural icon during the war. She represented the thousands of women who stepped up in extraordinary ways. They took on male-dominated jobs, like working in ammunition factories and shipyards. The irony is that Rosie earned her place in a male-dominated society that, if not for the war, would not readily allow her to pursue her talents in those fields.

It is important to recognize that when women are pressured to compromise their authentic selves, strain is put on the whole of society, including men. It happens in much the same manner as when any discriminatory practices are allowed to persist unchallenged. In contrast, wherever diversity and individual freedoms are embraced and cared for, growth and prosperity thrive.

BELIEVING AND BE LIVING

The way to develop a strong personal code of ethics is to clearly define what it is you *believe*, and then *live* that every day, fearlessly and fundamentally. I like to say, "Believing and be living." Live what you believe.

Doing the right thing can be difficult. Cutting corners and taking the low road is tempting because it often appears to be an easier way to go. So in moments of decision, I encourage you to draw strength from whatever source works for you. Many people put their faith in God or a higher power. I know parents who summon strength by thinking about their children, envisioning the better world they want their children to inherit. Find what works for you and stick with it.

JANICISMS

START OUT THE WAY YOU CAN END OUT

One day, shortly after Bernie and I were married, I was on the third-floor balcony of our beach home talking with my mom, and I said, "Oh, I have to go down and get some coffee for Bernie."

She gave me a wise but disapproving look and said, "Start out the way you can end out."

I looked at her, puzzled.

She continued, "It'll be a lot better to never get him a cup of coffee for the first three months of marriage, and then, after the first three months, get it for him every day the rest of your life. He'll think it's a treasure and a treat. But if you start out doing it, he's going to always expect it, and he'll wonder what went wrong when you stop."

After I thought about it, I recalled that she did everything for Daddy, and he always reacted like it was the most amazing, magical moment. There's a lot of wisdom in that saying: start out the way you can end out.

At the core of my personal brand, as I've mentioned before, is the devout belief that I must never compromise who I am personally to become who I wish to be professionally. It's a way of life for me, and we teach this to all of our executives. I did not develop this core value overnight. It took years. It was a process. I am still growing, learning, and refining, not just in the realm of ethics, but in all areas of life. You, too, may find that your ethical journey lasts a lifetime.

KEY WISDOM AND INSIGHTS

- Always behave as if what you do in the dark will come to light. Act as if you're always on camera.
- Don't run down competitors; talk from your strength.
- To thine own self, and to others, be true. If your conscience is telling you that it's not comfortable with your actions, you need to course correct.
- Wherever diversity and individual freedoms are embraced and cared for, growth and prosperity thrive.
- Whatever you believe, live it fearlessly and fundamentally every day.

⟡

CHAPTER SIX

Pressure Makes Diamonds

THE LATE SUMMER SUNLIGHT GLINTED OFF THE green collards. The plants were so shiny their heavy wet leaves appeared to be twinkling like diamonds. And when Mama cooked, she prepared them so perfectly that they were as hearty as a T-bone steak.

We had a beautiful year-round garden where we grew tomatoes, squash, peppers, corn, cabbage, peas, and herbs. Daddy insisted that we learn, and fully understand, what it takes to put food on the table. We kept spring, summer, fall, and even winter gardens. Of all the vegetables in the garden, those pesky cucumbers were my least favorite to pick. I still flinch every time I think about that awful feeling of my hands getting pricked by the thorns on their skin. But the reward of having fresh cucumbers sliced and served with salt and pepper or with Mama's homemade tangy vinegar and sugar sauce made it worth the effort.

My mother would always make sure I got the first serving. I suspect that she was silently rewarding me for doing the thing that I hated most. What this also did was teach me the direct relationship of work ethic to outcomes. Gardens do not tend themselves. They require consistent care and dedication. Anything worth having does. You won't win results unless you battle the seasons to work the soil, plant the seeds, and tend your garden, no matter what it is you're trying to grow.

DISCIPLINE IS NOT A DIRTY WORD

My adult life and career have provided many lessons on work ethic. But it was during my childhood that I learned the truth of six words that I have coined as a mantra and lived by throughout my entire career: discipline is not a dirty word.

A lot of people seem to treat it as such. Most people get preprogrammed somehow to think that by disciplining themselves to do work, they must necessarily be giving up something more enjoyable. They come to dread self-discipline because they focus on the wrong thing.

Instead of focusing on the positive results they'll achieve if they do the work, they focus on the fun activity they're missing out on. The typical thinking goes like this, "I really need to work on my business this weekend. But I'd rather go to the beach. Ugh! I wish I could go to the beach. The beach would be so fun. I'm missing out on the beach." This person is focused on the beach, beach, beach.

This is backward thinking. It's the exact opposite of what you should be thinking about—the positive results that will come from doing the work. Change your mindset from beach, beach, beach, to, "I know that if I do the work, then this desired result will happen. I'll feel great when it does." Can you remember the children's story *The Little Red Hen*?

By going to the office instead of the beach, you're making an investment in your life. You're getting closer to your desired outcomes. You'll have a sense of satisfaction and accomplishment as you work toward your goal. Those are all worthwhile accomplishments with corresponding positive emotions. Focus on the outcome.

In contrast, if you go to the beach you'll feel *guilty* for wasting the day when you could have been productive. So, the way I see it, you're not *giving up* having fun at the beach, you're *gaining* progress toward your desired outcome. After a short period of progress and reward, you may even take technology in hand and make the shore-side your office!

DISCIPLINE IS MY ANGEL

Self-discipline you own. Self-discipline isn't federally regulated. It isn't taxed. You don't need anyone's permission. It doesn't depend on anyone but yourself. I remember my trainer telling me, "You never resent the workout you just had, but you often regret the one you didn't do."

Discipline has been my own personal angel in life. The ability to decide to do things deliberately that will assure me of reaching my goal has been my greatest strength. Discipline is more important than *what* you know or *who* you know. Discipline is about the *how—how* much and *how* many.

I am proud to say that my ability to apply myself toward a desired outcome has enabled my success. To apply myself *by myself*. Whether it's discipline in how I eat, or getting my exercise, or taking action toward reaching a defined business goal, it's always been discipline that won the day. Self-discipline is not something to be feared or struggled with or "worked at." It's not about sacrifice. You get to see who you really are and how much you really want it by how disciplined you're prepared to be.

I've just never understood why people torture themselves with, "I can't have that. I can't eat that. Well...maybe I'll have just a little piece." That never made sense to me. I've always thought, "I don't want that *because* I want this." They don't live in the same place. I think, "I don't care what it tastes like, it can't get me the result I'm after, so why would I want it?"

It's a waste of energy when people twist themselves into an inner debate, asking, "Should I or shouldn't I?" I remember being puzzled by classmates in high school who hated going home and doing their homework. I wanted the grades, I needed the scholarship. So I *wanted* to go home and study because I *needed* the result. Homework was always first in line for me. I love being on my grind, knowing what I'm going to get from it, knowing what I need to put into it, and then doing those things to make it happen.

HUMANS ARE BUILT FOR WORK

The great thing about being a human is that we get to design our work. Each of us gets to determine how we spend our time and our days. Some people like to relax and take naps; others prefer to work hard. Where the real dispute comes in is the *meaningfulness* of work, the purpose of work and the value of work.

Meaningfulness can incorporate different criteria for different people. These might include self-fulfillment, humanity, purpose, immediate outcome, long-term plan, or strategic outcomes. What is meaningful and fulfilling to one person might be total drudgery and boredom to someone else.

So what does all this mean to a person? It means that in the end, you do get to design what your life is about or what your work is about. If your work is not fulfilling, it's on you to make a change. Maybe that means going back to school to complete an education or get a graduate degree. Maybe it means getting a different job. While you may have a few jobs on the way to a career, all of this work and the approach that you take to it really does influence the outcome for you as a human being.

Why is it that people who are doing fulfilling work that they enjoy and that they're proud of feel better, are more fulfilled, and enjoy life more? Recently, I asked someone close to me who is semiretired what it felt like to be on a reduced work schedule. He said that when he's not at work, he feels depressed, and when he is at work, he feels exhilarated. It's my firm belief that human beings were built for work. We were not built to be idle or to relax on the beach. Everything about us biologically and psychologically indicates that functionally we're at our best when we can attach some input and output that's progressive.

The elemental aspects of being human dictate that work becomes a part of that. The disconnect for so many people, I believe, occurs when they find themselves or place themselves in an environment where they're not doing things they love in return for pay.

Too many people are stuck in a mentality of this idea that you work to earn the money, and that money, in turn, allows you to play. Very few people are being encouraged to find play in the work that earns them the money. Imagine a world in which we could all get paid for doing what we love to do. That's the world I live in and the one I want everyone reading this book to live in.

When people who love their work retire, sometimes they really slow down and begin to wither or just plain fall apart. That's something that a lot of people don't know. Most of the people I know are just working to get to retirement, and they forget that.

Too many people fail to properly save for and plan for retirement. While they're on their grind during their peak earning years, they're focused on enjoying themselves. They're taking all of these wonderful trips and doing fun things that maybe their community or their loved ones will celebrate them for. But then suddenly they find themselves in retirement without a substantial nest egg. Often, people are forced to accept a lower living standard in retirement than they had at the peak of their work performance all because they didn't plan for it.

One of the things that can be helpful, and I've seen it to be helpful to some who've done it, is to start asking yourself the questions about your retirement that you would love to have had the opportunity to ask others you love about theirs. What are your financial plans? Where do you want to live? Do you have a contingency plan? Many people don't plan a retirement or factor in reduced mobility or a changed health issue for themselves. By that I mean most of us envision old age to come simply with a slower pace or lesser vision. And I'm not speaking about business vision, I'm talking about twenty-twenty, edging its way up the chart. Very few people ask, "What if I get dementia or Alzheimer's? What if I incur some type of ailment that is rheumatic in nature?" These types of considerations completely change the game about whether finances alone are the primary consideration for retirement.

It's important for us to consider all of these factors. The goal is to have a healthier view around our expectations of others and ourselves in retirement. This will, in turn, encourage us to go ahead and enjoy where we're living now and not wait for retirement before we really start living.

DON'T MAKE LISTS; MAKE IT HAPPEN

During a group visit to the Whitehouse, President Clinton once taught me a lesson about simplicity that I'll never forget. He said, "In government, we are always dealing with billions and even trillions of dollars. That's a lot of zeros. It gets confusing. So to keep it simple, just take the zeros off, do the math with the numbers 1–9, then add the appropriate zeros back on and make your decision." I thought that was genius. The lesson was clear. All those zeros can be distracting. Even out of school and especially when dealing with real-life decisions. So first, simplify, then make your decision.

As the founder and CEO of a multi-billion-dollar business, believe me, I have to deal with tremendous complexity and a lot of tasks. I'm busy from the moment I wake up until I go to sleep. Here's one of my simplicity secrets. I do not make to-do lists. I think to-do lists provide a false sense of accomplishment. "Look at all the pretty to-do lists I've created. Look at this new app I downloaded to track all my tasks." I don't believe in that. I believe in discipline and taking action.

My philosophy is simple. Don't make a list; just make it happen. Rather than writing lists down, I believe in just doing it. When you write lists down, it's like an excuse to procrastinate. "Now that it's on my to-do list, I won't forget about it, so I can come back to it later." Then guess what? It languishes on the to-do list for weeks without getting done. Your time and energy would be better spent just getting it done now.

I'm not saying to-do lists are bad or that you shouldn't use them. I know many highly effective executives who live by their to-do lists. I'm just pointing out that there is another, action-focused philosophy that can render lists useless. Rather than spending time and mental energy to create, manage, update, rewrite, copy, cross off, notate, and keep track of a list, I'd rather just do a task and be done with it.

Another philosophy I follow is to do the hardest thing first. If you know you have to have a difficult phone call with an unhappy client, the natural tendency is to put it off until the last thing. But that leads to negative mental energy and stress. Get the hardest tasks out of the way first. Then enjoy the rest of your day accomplishing the easier stuff.

I find discipline and doing it now to be very freeing and

exhilarating. There's nothing better than designing a process to achieve an outcome, then executing the process with discipline, and then achieving the outcome.

STAMINA VS. STICK-TO-ITIVENESS

Stick-to-itiveness and stamina are not the same thing. Stick-to-itiveness is attitude driven. You've got an attitude of staying in it to win it. Stamina is the physical and mental ability to do all the things that come with that attitude.

The distinction is important. Just because you really, really want to do it doesn't mean that you will do it. We've all seen examples of that in our own lives. You need to make sure that you are mentally and physically resourced to succeed. You must check in from time to time to make sure that you're doing what you need to do so that you can achieve your goal. Building up your stamina will keep you going and doing what you need to do. Even if your mental agility is crisp and on point and you want to stick with it, if your stamina is low, it won't allow you to get the work done.

It's also a good idea to have someone whose opinion you value to tell you the clear truth about how they see you, and not just how you see you. Often, through no ill intention, we may view ourselves as stronger in certain areas than we really are. Or we may read ourselves more negatively. An independent opinion is helpful now and then to keep us on track and make sure we're maximizing our stick-to-itiveness and our stamina.

USE A VISION BOARD

One of the things that can support the stamina for someone going after a goal is visioning and vision boards. In my organization, we encourage teams to succeed by creating individual vision boards that they share in a team environment. Then we compile some of those key elements into a team vision board. Our team members find a lot of support from one another.

One of our branches in Texas determined that not only would they do vision boards individually and as a team, but also, each person put on their desk a picture frame with one or two things they're envisioning. Then they determine the number and volume of sales that they will need to achieve in order to reach that goal. Each person in that office has a buddy to whom they are accountable. For ten minutes a day or less, they talk about their vision, how they're progressing toward achieving it, what's necessary, what they need to tweak or adjust, and how to go about doing it.

A big part of that team vision is to be invited to attend our company's annual Founders' Club celebration. Every year, we invite everyone who achieves certain predetermined results on an all-expenses paid trip where we wine them and dine them and show our gratitude for a job well done. Last year was Jamaica; this year it's the Dominican Republic. In the past, it's been Hawaii or Mexico. In addition to a good time, Founders' Club is a chance to network with one another, share best practices, and celebrate their accomplishments. We have a tremendous gala night, where the employees are honored on stage, and the red carpet is rolled out for them. That's a big win for an office, and it's a big win for individuals. Many choose to bring their kids or significant other and just enjoy being celebrated.

Each office I've visited in the last four months has a big vision board hanging up in their employee lounge area with pictures of next year's Founders' Club destination. And they've written out the goal they need to reach as a team and incorporated a thermometer to graphically illustrate their progress toward that goal.

It's exciting to see the team build around this. Yes, it's worth it to envision your way to a dream vacation. But what's more important is that before they earn that vacation, as an office, many of them are earning the things that matter to their significant others, their family, and their community.

Sometimes, it's a gift to a community charity that they are planning. Sometimes, it's a school that they want to support, attend, or send a child to. Most of the time, it's about earning something that's important to somebody else that has to be achieved before they reach Founders' Club. So by the time they come to Founders', tremendous accomplishment has already been made. Time after time, I learned from Founders' attendees, it's those vision boards that really help to get them there.

My vision board is present with me wherever I go. Because I travel so much, every time I turn on my iPad, I have my vision board present. It serves as my screensaver. My vision board is also hanging up and framed very nicely in my closet. It's my personal space that I go to when I need to be me in a very defined way. My vision board is a great reminder of why I'm doing what I'm doing. Some people find areas in their home that they dedicate for a vision board. Others may keep it in a box in the trunk of their car and look at it every time they open their trunk. For me, it's really important to have it present in intentional and unintentional moments. It keeps my courage up where I need it to be to achieve the things I'm aspiring to.

It's very important to distinguish between what the company goals are and what your personal goals are that you put on your vision board. They could be the same from time to time, but what is important is to understand that the company's goal may be $100,000 in sales. Your personal vision board may be the house that you've eyed that you'd like to buy.

Underneath that house are the transactions, their values, and timelines that are necessary in order to reach that goal, and one of those may be the company's goal. If the company says unless you sell a hundred thousand you're no longer employed, likely it's going to be under that vision.

On the vision board, usually, is a picture or a quickly worded outcome that you wish to achieve. On my vision board is a picture that has a person in it who matters to me. And around it are the things that need to be achieved in alignment with what that picture represents to me. Your vision board should display the things that matter behind why you're doing something. It's really important to have those images visually in front of you.

PRESSURE MAKES DIAMONDS

It always amazes me how people can go through adversity or affliction, then somehow come out stronger on the other side. That's what I'm talking about when I say pressure makes diamonds. My husband is a good example.

Bernie grew up in Yorkshire, England. He was about ten years old during World War II. It was one of the most difficult periods in history, especially for British families, and especially in the early years of the war before America entered the fight against Hitler. The men were off battling the Nazis. And the women and children were holding down the home front. Meanwhile, German air raids dropped bombs on civilian populations almost every night.

Bernie remembers how the government rationed food supplies. His mother was told how many eggs the family was legally allowed to have per week. British soldiers pulled up the railroad tracks in his neighborhood and the iron porch rails from his house so that the metal could be used for bullets and weapons. Bernie had to leave school in the fourth grade, as did many children who lost male teachers because they were off fighting in the war. Bernie worked in his own little victory garden. Many English families avoided starvation by supplementing their rations with food bought illegally on the black market and/or keeping victory gardens. These gardens were not always kept as singular family or individual decisions. Many English communities organized their efforts around keeping collective gardens and sharing the produce.

It was a very dark and difficult time. Nearly half a million people from the United Kingdom died in the war. An estimated sixty million people died worldwide. Bernie and his family suffered a lot. But I think he became a stronger, more disciplined, harder worker and a more positive person because of the discipline his mother taught him and the trials and hardships he went through. Bernie is well into his 80s now, and he still gets up every day before 6:00 a.m. and is out the door to go to work. I admire him so much. As a matter of fact, his intense desire to learn and his passion for work are among the top reasons I was so initially attracted to him.

Pressure really does make diamonds.

Here's why diamonds are a suitable metaphor for how going through difficult times makes people grow and become more effective. Diamonds are the hardest naturally occurring substance found on earth. But they're made from very common stuff—carbon. When carbon undergoes intense pressure for a long period of time, it eventually turns into diamonds. As we all know, diamonds are extremely valuable and prized all over the world. They are so prized that they have come to signify purity and strength and are often the stones of choice for wedding rings. They last forever, even if the marriages don't!

Similar to the way diamonds become very valuable after being under intense pressure, the same can be said of people. Entrepreneurs and business owners often undergo trial by fire and incredible stress, especially during the early years of forming and growing a company. After learning to battle with and navigate through intense pressure, they come out the other side stronger, wiser, more capable, and more experienced, which makes them exceedingly valuable. Just like a diamond. Pressure develops valuable positive character traits, including persistence, optimism, resilience, strength, fortitude, and resourcefulness.

I have found that employees and executives who have battled difficult times and survived, tend to have more depth and capability than people who have never truly been tested. Without fighting through intense pressure or overcoming difficult obstacles, one might remain soft, shallow, or superficial. I've been through too many battles to remember, some I wish I could forget. But I'm much stronger and more capable as a result. Pressure really does make diamonds.

RAISING A FAMILY AND A BUSINESS

Many of the women who approach me at conferences or after speeches ask me about work-life balance. It's a difficult subject. Some of the most successful women tend to struggle with some of the least successful home lives. My answer, as always, is direct and honest. I tell them, "You can have it all. But maybe not all at one time."

Growing a business and growing a family at the same time is a challenge for both genders, but particularly for women. For me, the idea of building a family brought many fears before it brought joy. The importance of family to me demanded that I become a mother in a way that emulated my own mother. I started to think about how I would create the nurturing environment my mother had and nurture and grow a business at the same time.

My mother worked from the home until my father passed away. When we returned home from school each day, Mama was either standing with her arms open to greet us, or tapping her foot, upset that we'd not shown up on time. Either way, we felt loved. How was I going to create an environment for my children that suggested a mom waiting with open arms every time they came home?

When my children were very young, many of the women who I knew in my professional and social circles would refer to the importance of spending "quality time" with the kids. I always wondered why you had to segregate time in terms of quality. Does that mean there's time that's not quality? For me, all time spent with my children is quality and has value.

Growing a family and growing a company at the same time was a constant battle. It was also joyous and demanding. Every moment was so special. Even though I worked a lot, I learned to cherish the unique value of each moment. That made it all worth it.

Today, our children really respect what we do and enjoy being a part of it, and neither of them is looking to be apart from it. They are talented and educated enough to do whatever they choose. For me, that's really been important. Our children are the greatest blessing in my life. Period!

CONFERENCE CALLS WHILE FLIPPING PANCAKES

I grew up in a home where meals were cooked with love for each other and gratitude for what we had. The kitchen was the family center. We would gather for discussions in the kitchen. We would solve problems in the kitchen. We would express hopes and make promises in the kitchen. We even prayed, sang, and saved souls in our kitchen. After daddy bought our big house across the street from our school, we still kept the kitchen sparkling white with yellow accents. Today, the kitchens in each of my homes are sparkling white with yellow accents. Any wonder?

Most people would think that a woman who is on the road three weeks out of a month, who works with the intensity and at the level that I need to in order to support my business, would find it a luxury *not* to have to cook when she gets home. But not me. I love to cook. I enjoy cooking each portion of a meal for my family. If I absolutely have to, I can hold a conference call or make business decisions while flipping pancakes. Often, I've actually done just that.

THE ART OF BERNIE
THE ART OF GROWTH

I have always given a lot of thought to why some people succeed in life while others struggle. The realization has come to me during repeated studies of *The Art of War*. Ability is an important part of one's success. However, it is second to an attitude of hunger to pay the price for achieving what is actually available to everybody yet claimed by only a few.

As you match your performance to the principles of *The Art of War*, you do not need to be literally as ruthless as is taught in physical warfare. However, you do need to perform with precision, passion, and profit, and be prepared to accept the responsibility so critical to leadership and success.

—BERNIE

When I was growing up, we had a big old table that would seat fourteen people. Folks dropped by all the time to say hi and share a meal. It wasn't unusual to have three or four visitors drop in over the course of a single meal. They'd share news from the community or ask for prayers for some loved one or themselves. The kitchen became a significant place for me that was nurturing, healing, and joyous.

It was also a safe place to be open, revealing, and vulnerable. I wanted to make sure I captured that same spirit in my kitchen for my own children. That's the environment I was brought up in, and however many zeros there are on the end of my paycheck, I wanted to recreate it. Today, whenever I arrive at one of my homes, whether in Las Vegas, California, North Carolina, or England, I jump out of my clothes and throw on a onesie. (Yes, a onesie—don't judge.) Then I light my candles, adjust my yellow flowers just so, and start to cook.

If it's not mealtime, I cook, and I freeze it in to-go boxes. I just love to cook. Period. When I get home and I'm in my kitchen, my mind is in a place where I can think and just "do me." I think about things related to my business. I talk with people who I treasure or people whose opinions I value. Most often, however, I arrive home late in the evening, so I cook in solitude, where I can just listen for God, quietly, without interruption.

It's bliss. Cooking may not be your thing; but please find yours if you don't know it by now—and just "do you."

SUNDAY DINNERS

When Bernie and I decided to have children, he asked for one commitment of me, and I asked for one of him. The commitment he requested of me was that I not try to keep the kids quiet and neat. The commitment I requested of him was that our home not be used for business. While I've broken my promise a bit, we've only made exceptions to my rule once or twice in forty years. It was really important to me that home be home.

By the time we had children, I had enough distance from my childhood to recognize a lot of the strong values it offered me. One of those was that our home really was a nest, and I wanted that for our children. I know that some people have identified both my husband and me as workaholics. I don't choose that as a description for myself. I know that being fully engaged with my kids is mandatory, not just my pleasure.

Family has been important to me in a deeply intense way. I breastfed my son until he was almost four years old. I wanted children for all the wonderful reasons you have children. I believed they deserved a home where they could be whole and innocent. A home where we would bring our best selves to their new lives.

I gave birth to both of our children at home because Bernie and I wanted to fill out their birth certificates ourselves. My husband is a Norman Saxon, Yorkshire-born white man. I'm an African American. If our children were born in the hospital, the nurse would write on the birth certificate "Mixed race." I hate it when society tries to label people, especially children.

Bernie and I decided that our children would not be raised as mixed; rather, they would be raised as members of the human race. So when we filled out their birth certificates, under the category of race, we wrote, "Human."

JANICISMS
CLEAN, HEALTHY FOOD IS THE
FUEL OF YOUR SUCCESS

Exercise is only part of what's required for a healthy mind, body, and spirit. You also have to eat right. Healthy, natural foods in moderate quantities multiple times a day are always better than bingeing on one or two high-calorie, high-fat meals.

Think of it this way. You wouldn't run an expensive sports car on the cheapest, lowest quality gasoline you could find, would you? No way. Your body is a finely tuned machine capable of incredible things. Fuel it properly.

This same issue popped up again and again when Brett and Kay were school age. They had to fill out forms which asked if they were black, white, Hispanic, Asian, or whatever.

They literally would ask us, "Mom, do we choose mixed?"

And I answer, "You're not mixed. You're blended. You just draw a line through all of that and write in the word 'human.'"

Today, our children are adults who are fully clear about themselves. They are equally clear that they are in a race for humanity.

As they grew older, we committed to spending weekends with family. Period. Saturday and Sunday are family time. Sunday evenings are reserved for family dinners at my house. We've been doing family dinner every Sunday for many years now. I cook all of it, from the main course to the sides. I don't even let people bring other dishes because it will mess up my table.

Every Sunday, we usually have around twenty people at dinner. Sharing a home-cooked meal is a wonderful way to stay connected and catch up. It's my way of honoring my commitment to keep weekends for family. Sunday dinners are a great blessing and something we all look forward to each week.

There have been significant opportunities and enticing requests that I've turned down over the years because I made that commitment. If you ever check my schedule, very rarely will you see me attend anything on a weekend without my family.

MY DAILY SCHEDULE

Many CEOs like to impress people with their tales of waking up at 4:30 in the morning, running six miles before work, and staying at the office until late at night. Well, that's a good story. But I'm a CEO, and I just don't think that works well for me.

My daily schedule is designed to support the leadership I need to provide to my company, as well as my social and family responsibilities. Sleep has never been a thing I needed or wanted much of. For me, sleep is like dying a miniature, temporary death at the end of every glorious day. I'm not a fan. Yet I do understand that my body needs it. The difficulty I have every day is to discipline myself to go to sleep.

My business travel schedule is demanding. Since we have operations in twenty-plus countries, I sleep more nights in hotels than I do at home. Sticking to a daily routine with set times for activities just isn't practical. Every day is different, partly because I'm usually in a different time zone.

JANICISMS
STAY HEALTHY ON THE ROAD

Traveling for business forces you to be creative about keeping fit. When I'm in a great walking city, which many are, I attempt to walk as much as possible, whether from meeting to meeting or after a day's work. When this is neither possible nor optimum, I use the hotel gym or get creative in my room. Bottles of water tied to my ankles while doing sit-ups, anchoring my feet under beds to do exercises, or just doing plain planks have me process the day's anxieties and pass into calm.

The routine in my life is made up of the things I do, but not the patterns in which I do them. For example, at least once per day, I'm guaranteed to have a quiet moment of gratitude. I live in deep thankfulness. When I wake up every morning, I'm filled with it. No matter where I am, I share a moment with the universe and with my creator to be appreciative. I never put words to it. For a long time, I did put words to it. But now, I just sit, and I open up in gratitude.

I give most of my time management attention to scheduling weekends so I can be home to enjoy family. We're very lucky that our adult children live nearby. I treasure my time with them, and that commitment is important.

HEALTH MUST BE A TOP PRIORITY

Every business owner should take their personal health as something that is an expectation and an offering to more than just themselves. It's common sense that you want to be healthy for yourself and for your family, but I think it's also common practice that you should be healthy based on the fact that others are depending on you to make decisions that impact their livelihoods. People who are employed by you need you at your best every day.

You can often see the health of a leader exhibited through the health of the organization simply by how well the company is performing. So it's just a good practice. It's a good personal practice, but it's smart business to keep yourself healthy. Some business owners work sixteen hours a day and neglect their health, eat bad food, and don't exercise; that is actually putting the company and their employees at risk in a way that they should not be.

We've seen many times when a business owner who holds so much of the decision-making, or the relationship building is not in good health or has some negative impact in their lives that changes the course for that business. And that's unfortunate for everyone in the organization. There are already enough external things out there that can negatively impact any business, but you shouldn't add to those risks by not taking care of yourself.

Today, as I look at my own health, I understand two key things. One, a lot of people are dependent on me making healthy decisions and being healthy in my own person. And two, I have the tremendous blessing of a daughter and a son who are very engaged in healthy living themselves. So living in the spirit and in the environment of a healthy family certainly supports me to be able to maintain those standards that I set for myself. They don't just include how I eat but also how I feed my mind.

We all get our results from where we place our attention. You can apply this to how you approach health as well. So if we're attentive to making sure that we eat in the way that we get the best energy and makes us healthier, then that's going to deliver the results we want. This also applies to whether we are getting the rest we need. For me, sleep is like miniature death, so I have to remind myself to sleep as a responsibility, not as a pleasure. For some people, sleep is an absolute pleasure, and it's the crown in the jewel of their day. Not me.

When it comes to working out, certain exercises work better for me than others. Exercises that also get in stretching and that allow me to spend time with other people are the ones I enjoy most. Walking is a good one. But weight-lifting and running exercises are not really for me, so getting exercise in the company of my son is going to be very different than in the company of my daughter.

But the main thing is that I'm on the road so much, so I've had to learn to adapt exercise that works for me to the conditions of my heavy travel schedule. Sometimes, that means I lay a towel on the floor and stick my ankles up under a bed and do my lifts, or I do my twists. Sometimes it means that I use bottles of water instead of weights like I do in my own gym at home. The point is that I've figured out how to adapt exercise for myself when on the road. Even on the airplane, if it's just to make sure that I'm keeping my blood circulating, I will do exercises with my feet and my arms. That can sometimes invite different kinds of conversation from people because I don't fly private. It's always worth it once I reassure the person seated next to me that I'm not going to do anything strange on a plane.

Sometimes I've even had passengers join me and say,

"Thank you. That was a great little workout." It's all about how you approach health and how you approach others that you are going to be able to be successful with this. The bottom line is that it's important to find a way to exercise no matter what your situation and that you can get it done and that you can create fun ways to do it for yourself. Sometimes it takes a little creativity.

The moment you stop taking care of yourself, that's the moment when you start the decline of your business unless control of that business is being transferred into the hands of someone who is taking care of their health. That can be an option for you, but why work that hard and not be able to enjoy the outcome? That business deserves you healthy every day that you're in a position to lead it.

Employees pay attention to what the leader of an organization does, including how he or she treats their own body. In particular, if you are the owner or the leader of a smaller business, you have much more visibility to your employees than say someone who leads a giant corporation. You can set a standard for how people behave and how people perform. You never have the right to put that on them, but you always have a responsibility to influence them in the best possible way.

I've seen companies where when the leader or the owner takes on a certain exercise regime, it becomes popularly known within the organization. What happens every time? Others will follow that lead. We've all seen how someone who looks great today, who maybe didn't have that level of energy or wear that certain size of outfit two months ago gets a lot of questions about what happened and what created the change. A leader is going to be observed and followed, whether people are asking out loud or not. So it makes good sense to show up in your best health every day, not just in your best dress.

YOUR BUSINESS IS YOUR FAMILY (BUT IT'S REALLY NOT)

I've heard many entrepreneurs and business owners say, "My company is my child. I created it and raised it. I watched it grow. Now my employees are like my family members." I can totally see where that idea comes from. I understand the sentiment. I think I've said the same things at times in my career because there is wisdom in it. In many ways, the founder of a company is like the head of a household.

But only to a point.

I suspect the entrepreneurs who say, "My business is my child," probably have not yet had actual human children of their own. Any parent will tell you that having children will show you a deeper realm of love, care, and devotion than you ever thought possible. All entrepreneurs are devoted to their businesses, but having a child is a different experience.

When we have children, we hold them, we support them, we prepare them, and we go to battle for them with the expectation that they will grow up one day and we won't need to do that anymore. Some parents even think, or expect, that their children will grow up and then, in turn, go to battle for *them* in their old age.

My view is that your business and your career are extremely important. But everything is relative. You must be prepared for your perspective and priorities to change when you get married and have a family of your own.

I encourage you to pursue your entrepreneurial dreams with all the hard work and dedication you can muster. But entrepreneurship and building a company can put stress on personal relationships and make it difficult to have a balanced life. Remember to prioritize the people who give your life meaning and satisfaction over your business.

KEY WISDOM AND INSIGHTS

- Discipline is not a dirty word. Self-discipline is more important than what you know or who you know.
- Don't make a to-do list, just take action and do it.

When you write to-do lists, it's like an excuse to procrastinate.

- Pressure makes diamonds. When people go through adversity, they usually come out stronger on the other side.
- Women in the workplace can have it all, but maybe not all at one time.
- Your company might be your child, but only until you have children.

CHAPTER SEVEN

Jump!

IT WAS A FRIDAY AFTERNOON. MOST PEOPLE WERE wrapping up their work and planning to head off for some much-needed rest and relaxation after a long week. The phone rang. Little did I know that one phone call would change the course of our company and lead to massive growth for years to come.

But it didn't sound like an opportunity at first. It sounded like an enormous problem. *Not* what we wanted to deal with on a Friday afternoon.

We were a backup vendor for a large Silicon Valley tech company that used hundreds of temporary workers. As a backup vendor, we supplied about 5–10 percent of the staffing needs. The primary vendor supplied the other 90 percent. We both worked under the same SLAs (Service Level Agreements) and pricing structure. In order to make a profit as a lower-volume backup vendor, we designed technology to help us be more efficient, faster, and more precise in how we delivered. We had to maximize our efficiency because the cost of doing business couldn't exceed the pay.

On that Friday afternoon, the Silicon Valley company called us and said, "The primary vendor is screwing us. Bad. We had a dispute, and they pulled out all their temps and left us with a mess. We're in trouble. Please help us." They were in big trouble because the dispute meant their temps weren't being paid, and there is a huge penalty for not paying workers. They wanted us to fix it.

So Trish, my brother Carlton (our account manager), Roni (we called her "Roni the Rebel"), and I grabbed our laptops, went straight to the airport, and boarded a plane to Silicon Valley. During those days, we could still walk up to an airport counter and buy a ticket, board a plane in Los Angeles with no TSA agents present, and land in Northern California, all within an hour.

We worked all weekend to straighten out their problems, get all of the temps paid on time and in the right amounts, make sure the legal paperwork was updated, and get the staffing operation running smoothly again. We had to move those employees, who elected to, from working for

the other staffing agency to working for us; you can't just
send a check. It's our bank account, so they had to technically and legally work for us. We had to sign up all those
workers in order to pay them. We also had to assume all
the liabilities, the risk, and everything else to get them
paid. It was a big gamble.

We did all this in three days by implementing our pro-
prietary processes and our own custom-built computer
software solution that we had developed in-house. We
sorted everything out over the weekend, fixed the problems, and got them back up and running. Before we left
on Sunday night, we generated and printed a full report
describing everything we had done. We left it on the desk
of the director of human resources. Problem solved.

The following Monday, I received a call from the company's HR director. I thought she was angry because her voice was so high-pitched, and she was hyperventilating. When she calmed down, I understood. She said, "How on earth did you guys do in one weekend what we haven't been able to get the primary vendor to do in twelve years?" They had not gotten proper reporting. They didn't have job descriptions lined up with pay, and a ton of important data and necessary reports were missing.

She was fascinated that we'd done it so well and so fast. "That's how we run our business," I replied. "That's what we do." They were so impressed by what we had accomplished, they actually tried to buy the system that we used to generate that information.

We thought about selling it to them. Carlton is a very caring and astute businessman. He said, "JBH, if they want it that bad, why don't we keep it?" I knew then and there that our next business had been born. Carlton's question helped me to identify that potential opportunity. My entrepreneurial instincts suggested, "Don't sell our *technology* to them. Encourage them to buy our *service*." That's how AgileOne one was born.

Based on that experience, we decided to invest heavily and turn it into an enterprise software product to roll out to clients around the country. It was a big risk because it required a lot of investment up front in time, resources, and money to build a new division of our company. But it turned out to be the right decision. AgileOne has evolved into our flagship brand. It literally changed the entire course of my company.

There are two lessons to take away from this story. First, we could have taken the safe route and sold the technology. But we assessed the potential and realized that our best move would be to invest in the technology and roll it out as a new product. We decided to jump. To roll the dice and take a calculated risk.

And second, we took a long-term view with an eye toward value creation. That one decision has created hundreds of millions of dollars in value for our clients and for our company. Entrepreneurs and intrapreneurs should always focus on value creation.

KNOWING WHEN TO JUMP

Taking risks is akin to knowing the right moment to jump across a busy street. There are, if we're lucky, street signs and traffic indicators that guide us before we step off the sidewalk. The obligation—and the opportunity—is ours to pay attention to the signs. Then we have to use our best judgment to know the right moment to cross that busy street.

MAMA SAYS
HASTE MAKES WASTE

This is an age-old saying that came along way before Mama. It is as true now as it ever was. What was unique and special is how Mama taught us this important lesson.

One of the most creative things I remember doing with my mom was sitting around making quilts. She taught us at a very young age how to cut up old clothes and sheets and give them a rebirth as beautiful hand-made quilts. I actually thought that's what she was teaching us when we were doing it. Remember, we were six girls sitting around with scissors, needles, and thread. But making the quilts wasn't the lesson; it was everything she taught us through the stories and the themes we talked about during those long sessions.

When we were cutting squares, Mama would say, "Wait a minute, wait a minute, slow down now. The most important thing you're going to do right now is cut the squares perfectly. If you don't, nothing will fit into place, and we're going to have to go back and start over." Because when you cut the squares, the quality of the squares determines the size and the correctness of the whole quilt. When we would hurry and not get it right, we'd have to go back and undo all those stitches. It resulted in wasted material, wasted energy, and wasted time. Lesson learned.

Businesses are like that in many ways. An established company is like the walk along a sidewalk that is safe. It gets you where you want to go on the path you know is predictable; by your own effort, you arrive there with little risk. But at some point, you want to cross the street to reach new customers. You want to go into new geographic areas and new vertical markets, and you want to launch new product offerings. All of those things involve risks. So you have to assess the available information and make a strategic decision to jump.

ASSESSING RISK

After that Silicon Valley company offered to buy our process, we had to decide whether or not we would continue to be a staffing company only or whether we would offer something bigger, better, and more valuable to our clients. One evening, my mother and I were speaking, and I shared my worry about whether we'd ever attract any large, brand-name clients.

At the time, we were doing close to sixty million dollars in business with our retail clients, and they remain very close to my heart. Retail clients are companies who buy our staffing services one person at a time or one solution at a time, maybe only once a year or maybe thirty people in a year. Retail clients are not those giant companies with whom you sign hundred-page contracts. Those huge companies were attractive to me. If we could get some of those huge contract clients, we could grow the business exponentially. But it would come with a lot more risk.

We had to decide whether we were going to invest a lot of money into the technology. That was the key. It would be a huge risk to hire so many programmers. Many nights, I sweated it out. It was necessary for me not to let fear overwhelm me as I was making the jump. There had been indicators along the way that it was the right time. But it was also important not to allow my desire to grow to cloud my judgment.

Working from the gut does have its value. In my opinion, gut is your own personal thermometer. But you've still got to pay attention to the temperature of the water before you jump in, just as you've got to pay attention to the traffic before you step off the sidewalk.

Our willingness to risk hiring a technology team to build out that new product paid off. The software eliminated geographic limitations for my business. We could now grow globally. The technology took me into the cloud, and that led to expansion into more than a dozen countries.

INTERNATIONAL RISK

That expansion brought a whole new level of risk: the risk of owning businesses in other countries. A friend of mine said to me, "Janice, you're doing so well, and you're cute, but you're not getting any younger. Why are you picking this moment to grow your business into countries that haven't proven to be friendly to business? Why are you going into France?"

It was a fair question. Our French lawyer told us, "You have to be strong-hearted to own a business in France if you are not French. But we will help you evaluate all your problems *before* you hang your sign and invest too much money. We won't bring all these problems to you *after* you're in business."

He continued, "In your country, you can open a business overnight, and then the problems show up. You find out later which laws you've broken. In France, we tell you all about it up front, so once you sign on the dotted line, you're signing it aware of what the opportunities and the threats are."

I thought about what he said. I had debated long and hard about opening my company in France. But to this day, his comments proved to be good advice. We did have a very detailed process that we followed before opening the business in France. That process identified potential risks that we could think through prior to being in business there.

When launching anything new, being clear about what the goals are is very important. Being clear about what the risks are is equally important. I expect there will be many more risks that I will have to face and many more opportunities to jump into. I believe that French lawyer gave me great advice. Identify all the challenges that you can anticipate first, match those risks up against the opportunity, and from there, decide whether to stay safely where you are or to open your eyes and jump.

IF YOU'RE NOT STRATEGIC, YOU'RE NOT ESSENTIAL

A client in a blue-chip firm once said to me, "Janice, if you're not strategic, you're not essential." In other words, you're dispensable unless you're so necessary to the client's business that they can't function without you. We call that being a strategic partner. Business owners need to remember this principle, especially in the early days when they're trying to get and keep their first customers.

If you're not necessary to the strategy of a company, they can get rid of you at any time, for any reason, and replace you with one of your competitors. Customers are interested in meeting *their* objectives, not yours. If you don't understand how you create value for *them*, then you may be a supplier, but you'll never be a strategic partner.

How you become essential is unique from customer to customer. But a good start is to ask the customer a very strategic question. "Can you name anything we offer that you want and need that no one else can provide?" Another way to ask this is, "What are we doing for you that no one else can do?"

When you're in business, if your client can't easily identify something you're doing for them that they want or need, that only you can uniquely do, you're at risk of losing that business. You are highly dispensable. When the contract period comes up, don't be shocked if you find that they're putting it out to bid.

Another way to become essential is to ask what you could be doing *even better* and then do it. When I visit clients, I ask them, "If I were the fairy godmother of my company and I could grant you a wish, what would be on your wish list for what we're not doing?" Always remember that your value is specifically tied to the client's needs, the client's goals, and the client's objectives. If you can find a unique way to meet all of the client's needs, then there's no reason for them to look anywhere else.

The time to ask your customers what you could be doing better is not when there's a problem. The best time is when things are going great. You're meeting all your KPIs, you're fulfilling or exceeding the terms of your Service-Level Agreement, and the customer is happy. That's the time to dig deeper and ask what you could be doing *even better*. Ask, "What's on your wish list right now?" "What could we do more of or less of to make you even happier?"

It's important to note that you should never word your question, "What can we be doing better?" That implies something's not going well. Always ask it this way, "What can we be doing *even* better?" That implies that what you're doing already is good. Another one of my favorite Bernie stories is his little Q&A that goes like this. Q: When is the best time to show your spouse you love him or her? A: Before someone else does!

If everything is going great, and you're getting more and more business from a client, don't assume it's because the client considers you essential. Your volume may not be up because they decided to give you more business. Your volume might be up simply because their business is up and they needed more help. You still need to get in there and ask questions, even when your business with that account is growing.

THE RISK *TO* AND THE RISK *NOT TO*

The whole nature of business is risk. Without risk, there is no business. Risk is not something to be avoided at all costs. It's something that every entrepreneur must strategically navigate as they grow their business.

Unfortunately, a lot of employees and companies take the cover-my-butt mentality toward risk. "I don't want to do anything too risky because it might come back on me." But experienced businesspeople know that the riskiest way to operate a business is to never take any risks.

They enjoy acting up! Taking the safe route in business is a recipe for mediocrity.

There are thousands of kinds of risk. But there are two, in particular, I want to discuss here. There's the risk *to*, and there's the risk *not to*. It's important to be able to balance those.

The risk *to* do something includes all the time, money, and manpower needed to make it happen. It also includes the opportunity costs of allocating those resources to that project and away from something else. This type of risk requires you to be fully educated and, if you're determined to go forward, fully resourced.

The risk *not to* is a cost that I don't think many entrepreneurs fully value because it's hard to place an exact price on a missed opportunity. There are plenty of stories about investors who passed on investing in Facebook, Uber, Dropbox, Snapchat, and Airbnb. They accepted the risk *not to* do something, and they paid a dear price.

Both of these risks should be fully considered and weighed against each other before making a decision.

CLEAR COMMUNICATION REDUCES RISK

The power of technology, analytics, and management

systems has been invaluable in helping to grow my business while reducing risk as much as possible. Still, there are myriad types of risks present in building a business, and no one person assumes responsibility for all risk. So communication becomes very important. Today, some kid in a garage may be developing a new technology solution or platform that will disrupt everything we're doing now as novel, innovative. Knowing how to partner and aggregate technology is critical—especially if you're not a technologist.

Clear communication is essential to mitigate risk. This is especially true if you go to market in any form of partnership. I learned this lesson the hard way. Failing to fully communicate regarding a contract ended up costing my business $900 thousand. If we had just followed proper communication procedures, we never would have lost that money. It was a bitter pill to swallow, but I've never forgotten the lesson.

To avoid disasters like that, all companies need clearly defined communication strategies, processes, timelines, and roles. No matter how well resourced a company may be, without effective communication, it will be vulnerable in dealing with risk.

LISTENING REDUCES RISK

Although most of us have heard the phrase "a woman's intuition," few of us would leave the deployment of resources and people to mere intuition. I believe part of women's intuition comes from the fact that many women have learned to listen critically. Women learn how to patiently listen to what is said and also how to listen for what is *meant*. Discerning between the two is often what creates our opportunities and our edge.

Plenty of men are also excellent listeners, and I think that gives them an advantage over men who don't listen. One of the best people I know at active listening is my son Brett. As a child, he was always a very curious learner. He wanted to listen and absorb everything he could before he would speak. He continues to be that way as an adult. He'll say, "Okay, now I've listened to you, Mom. I've listened to you, Dad. Let me tell you what I think we should do."

Brett will often ask, "Has everybody said what they need to say? Has everybody asked their questions?" I don't remember ever teaching him that. I would love to think I did, but it appears he learned that skill all on his own. That's innately how he operates. He really listens out loud, and he's able to do this because he's not letting his own noise interfere with what somebody else is saying. He's not thinking, "What am I going to say next? I'm not really listening to you—I'm just waiting until you're done so I can talk."

Mama always used to say, "Listen before you talk, and think before you walk." Listen to what's going on. Make sure what you're saying is relevant to the moment and not just something you're throwing out there. If it's a point you want to make, then make it at the appropriate time. Timing is everything in communication.

THE FOUR CORNERS OF A CONTRACT

There is a concept in business called the four corners of a contract. This is something your mother or father probably didn't teach you. A lot of people who've run businesses successfully, especially small businesses, may have done so for a while before they actually had to face this truth.

The bottom line in any business deal is this: if it's not within the four corners of a contract, it likely will not hold up in court, and it will not be enforceable. Once you get into court, the only thing that matters is what's within those four corners of the contracts. So that means that agreements made in emails or oral agreements may not be binding on either party.

When you contract, you need to understand that you contract with companies, but you do business with people. This is a very different thing, and it's something that you need to separate. When we enter contracts with smaller businesses, we are usually negotiating with the people who we're actually going to be doing the business with, or with people who we like and who like us well enough to set the precedent for us to do business within that company. In a day-to-day fashion, we often place the contract in the drawer, or leave it in some file on a computer, and then we get about the business of doing business.

It's a good idea though, it's a good principle, and it's a great practice to always check in with that contract and make sure that if you're performing favors outside of the four corners, or if you're performing outside of timelines written in that agreement, that you go back to check that. Because if you ever end up in a legal situation, it's the four corners of the contract that are going to govern any decision-making and outcomes from disputes.

It's also important to note that the people with whom you do business today within the client company may not be the people you are doing business with a year from now. And if they're not there to support that any change to your performance outside of contracted language was done by authority, you could be in a big bale of trouble. For example, you may have had a common working agreement with somebody who is the main point of contact there, but if they leave the company, you've got to start over with someone new, and they may not see things that way. Or they may not remember it that way. So it's just a good thing that when the business changes, you amend the contract, and keep everybody happy and on the same page. What's in the four corners of the contract always rules.

KEY WISDOM AND INSIGHTS

- Entrepreneurs and intrapreneurs should always focus on value creation.
- If you're not strategic, you're not essential. If you can become a strategic partner to your customers, they'll be customers for life.
- Regularly ask your customers, "What can we be doing *even* better?"
- Clear communication reduces risk.
- People who are good listeners will have an advantage in business over people who are just waiting for their turn to talk.

- If it's important, make sure it's in the four corners of the contract.

CHAPTER EIGHT

Together We Win

WE ONCE WORKED WITH TWO CLIENT COMPANIES who were direct competitors to each other. Let's call them Company A and Company B. These two companies produced competing products that were sold to the same marketplace. The job orders we received from each company were very similar in description and required identical skillsets. The companies even paid within the same range of compensation for each job type.

But the applicants we supplied to each company were completely different types of people. An applicant would either fit in at Company A *or* at Company B but not both. These businesses could not have been more different in their corporate cultures, and hence in their requirements for talent. Our understanding of the nuances was what earned us their respect and continued business.

BUILDING A CULTURE

Growing a business to more than a billion dollars in revenue is not necessarily an extraordinary thing. It happens all the time, all over the globe. What I believe *is* extraordinary is managing a business to a mature, well-defined, cohesive, working culture.

To do this, everyone from the CEO to the salespeople to the back-office teams must take a stake in the mission, as well as the function of the business. Understanding what the company produces or what service it offers, and who its clients are, is what builds the revenue. But seeing coworkers and colleagues as clients is how we begin to build a culture.

To create a bona fide corporate culture, it's important to clearly define the relationship of the business to the people who make the business work. This is the connection between the offering, the customer, and the company's talent. Hiring the right people for each position is the foundation for both revenue and culture growth.

RESPECT WHAT YOU EXPECT

In my first book *The Art of Work: How to Make Work, Work for You!*, I discuss the importance of "respecting what you expect." Most people do not quit a job or leave a company only for money. Most leave because they do not feel supported in their daily work or goals. In other words, they don't feel respected.

Isn't this the same reason people leave personal relationships? Understanding that work is where people invest most of their time, energy, and passion should help us to value the importance of creating processes and a culture that respect this. If you don't want your employees to break up with you, treat them with the respect and support that are required to nourish any close, personal relationship.

OPERATE LIKE A T.E.A.M.

Creating a supportive work culture is not born from one gender or the other. It comes from the desire to build an organization where employees operate like a T.E.A.M.—Treat Everyone As Myself. When employees treat coworkers as their own internal customers, a positive culture begins to grow. But more is required.

Creating a culture also means that employees must feel the freedom to innovate, even if they occasionally fail. They must feel respected and valued enough to make mistakes without worrying about losing their job. Employees have to know that, while not encouraged, mistakes will be supported.

Building an effective culture also requires information to be shared freely with employees and goals to be defined clearly. Ideally, *good* employees are supported and encouraged to become *great*. If employees are properly motivated and incentivized to become great, the company will also become great.

Leadership isn't about the boss trying to be a rock star. It's about the boss investing confidence, resources, and skill into the people who she's leading so that *they* become the rock stars, not just allowing employees to act up but especially encouraging them to. Our hiring philosophy is that we find great people and then support and develop them to become superstars.

One of the ways we help employees feel respected and supported is by offering them upward mobility, opportunities for career advancement and income growth, and assistance in reaching their goals. For example, my company spends millions of dollars every year on employee development and education. We don't call it training; we call it development. I told them they can't call it training because you train animals and you develop people.

Every once in a while, someone will ask me, "But Janice, you spend all that money on employee development. What if the employee leaves the company?" I always respond by saying, "But what if they stay?"

I've never worried about the loyalty that my employees show to *me*, I have always focused on the loyalty that I can show to *them*. This has been the most important thing to me, and they recognize and appreciate that.

These cultural values are how we've built such positive morale and longevity among our employees. And proof of that is the large number of team members who have been with us for more than a decade—in some cases, multiple decades. This is practically unheard of in today's employment landscape, where most people bounce from job to job a dozen or more times throughout their career. Company-hopping is especially common among millennials, who tend to change jobs and even careers with greater frequency than previous generations.

MILLENNIALS GET A BAD RAP

I sit in so many meetings where millennials are talked about in a negative way. An employee of mine, with tears in her eyes, once said to me, "Why is it that millennials have become the new black? You know, like they're the group that now gets talked about behind their back in a negative way at the water cooler."

Some of the comments I hear about millennials are downright insulting. "They don't understand the culture of business. They believe that everything is owed to them.

They're entitled. They don't get why they need to be at a desk from 8:00 to 5:00 if they can do the same amount of work from 2:00 until 4:00 at the beach on a new piece of technology."

I'm usually the person who speaks up to defend millennials. I say, "Well, I'm a millennial too. That is if millennial is a mindset, instead of an age range. Because I agree with a lot of the things they believe." For example, if I can get all my work done in half the time while working remotely, then why should I have to come sit in the office?

I think it will move business forward to actually add some parts of the millennial culture into the culture of traditional business and the workplace. By the way, they're your customers. They're the biggest demographic. I believe millennials deserve much more respect than they receive. The truth is, I'm the most magnificently mature millennial you'll ever meet!

DON'T BE A RELATIONSHIP THIEF

Everyone knows how important networking and relationship building is. But there is a mistake you must avoid that I see people make too often, and I call it being a relationship thief.

One of the things that I've noticed people do is they get introduced to someone by someone else who has a really good relationship with the person they're being introduced to. Then they automatically try to assume that same level of relationship. Too often, I have people in my professional network come back to me and say, "This young man came to me and said he's a friend of yours and asked for my support on something."

Even though I may have invested less than two minutes introducing them in a social setting, that's just opening a door. You still have to build your own relationship over time. So when that person tries to invoke a level of relationship with someone that they have not earned, it becomes uncomfortable for the person I introduced them to. And that reflects poorly on me.

Relationship thieves are people who sponge off of polite introductions and then try to create immediate close relationships out of them. In other words, they try to cross-brand with me in a way that positions them in a positive light, even though they have not yet earned that relationship. It may have taken me ten years to build a working relationship of trust with someone, so it's insulting to think that can be duplicated in a two-minute introduction.

So what I often do, and I encourage other executives or professionals to do, is coach people before you introduce them to any of your relationships. Explain that after the introduction, the person is not open for immediate solicitation; the introduction is just that, and now that you have met the person, you must work hard to build your own relationship with them.

Let me give you an example. If someone says, "Oh, Janice, will you introduce me to Jack, the VP of purchasing at XYZ Corporation?"

I will candidly say to them, "Yes, I'll introduce you. To what purpose would you like to meet them?"

Then I'll explain to them any personal protocols I may understand Jack has. For instance, if I'm with someone who loves pictures, I might say, "Jack is not going to be open to you taking a selfie with him at this event, so I would encourage you under my introduction, please don't ask that." Or "I know you're looking to put on your event next month, but please don't solicit Jack as a speaker."

Many people don't think about this when they ask. They're not intentionally being rude, they simply don't understand the protocol for building networks. Or they may be so rushed in their own lives and their quest for success or their immediate need that they may accidentally overlook what is good old-fashioned etiquette in some instances, and in other instances actually breach protocols.

Another thing about building networks is that it's always a good idea to allow someone who you're interested in knowing better to learn a little bit about you beyond what you're able to tell them in that initial meeting. You can invite them to visit a website or talk with people who they may be impressed by who know you and can validate who you are. That certainly can help to speed a relationship.

In other instances, it's simply going to require allowing them to get to know you in their own time. Remember, they've got a whole world they're living in, long before they met you for that two minutes via a quick invitation or you walking up to them at an event. Sometimes, you just have to build a relationship the old-fashioned way, gradually over time. Again, that's where clarity comes in; you have to be clear on what follow-through will be required to move a conversation toward the next step. Close the conversation by saying, "This has been very helpful, and I really thank you for the advice (or the offer of support) you've given. What is the best way for us to communicate? Should I text, email, or would you prefer a letter with paper and ink?" Until you know someone really well, you can't know what their preferred form of communication is without asking them. Of course, follow-through should always include a thank you.

In networking, it's also important to understand that oftentimes in business, networking people have different cell phones for business than personal. You need to be clear on what number you are communicating with people on and that your communication is appropriate based on that. We live in a device-driven and device-supported society today, so it's important to invest in face-to-face time, and to understand how people want to be communicated with in an electronic age.

FREEDOM TO INNOVATE

While my organization does not encourage our employees to make careless mistakes, we do encourage them to be free to innovate and try new things. We make it clear that we understand that errors will occur along the road to discovery. We want them acting up.

This element of our corporate culture was tested recently when one of my executive support team members needed to make a big decision on her own. A crisis popped up during one of my travels abroad. I was in Europe and she was in Los Angeles, so there was a time difference of eight hours between us. She couldn't reach me, and she had to make an immediate decision.

We had invested a lot of time and money in preparing for a client-partnered event, and at the last minute, we needed to find a new supplier. The only supplier she could find who was available to step in at short notice was a small company that had never done a job of that scale before. My executive took the initiative and made the decision. The supplier gallantly accepted the work and, needless to say, failed spectacularly.

It was a disaster.

My executive was so distraught as she was describing to me what had happened. She had no solution and was tearful as she confessed to what she thought was a ship-sinking occurrence. I walked her back from her mental ledge. We determined that we would bring our client into the situation to collaborate on a solution.

Based on their scale and internal supplier pool, we were able to change the event from formal to classy casual, which allowed guests to arrive dressed as planned and to be surprised by the casual-fun environment. It was a successful forum-closing event, and everyone had fun. Some attendees even cut loose and kicked off their painful dress shoes.

It was no fun having to make a call myself from overseas to confess our situation to that client and ask for help. It's not fun today when the situation is brought up. But it did create a client-partner experience in which my company and theirs learned to trust each other even more and collaborate on winning together. This client continues to be very important to us to this day.

More importantly, my executive team member was able to experience the truth of our company credo—of allowing freedom to innovate. Whether this freedom is needed in decision-making, product development, or interpersonal exchanges, it's always good for employees to know that they can stretch their abilities, grow their competencies, make decisions, and find support in the process. Employees work much more innovatively when they know there is freedom to discover through making errors.

TEACH THEM AND THEY REMEMBER; INVOLVE THEM AND THEY LEARN

One of the big benefits of encouraging employees to innovate is that they try and learn new things. This helps them build experience, expand their competencies, learn from mistakes, and become better employees. That builds a stronger company.

In the Bible, it states if you give a man a fish he'll eat for a day, but if you *teach* him to fish, he'll eat for life. Kids will say, "Let me do it, let me do it myself." It's instinctive in humans that we know we'll learn better by actually trying something ourselves, rather than just being told how to do it.

You can explain to a child fifty times how to tie a shoe. You can show them YouTube videos. You can demonstrate it yourself. But until the child does it herself, she won't have learned it.

My nephew Cameron is a good example. When Cameron was a little boy, my sister babysat him. Aunt Trish is a professional auntie. One day Trish was making hot coffee, and Cameron wanted some. Aunt Trish kept saying, "No, you can't have any."

"Why Aunt Tish, why not?"

"It's too hot Cameron; it's too hot."

That didn't make sense to him. *I can't have coffee because it's hot?*

"No Aunt Tish, it's cold, it's cold!"

"Cameron, it's hot."

"No Aunt Tish, it's cold!"

They went through that over and over again, until finally, Trish said, "Well, have it!"

Cameron took a big sip.

"Aunt Tish, it's hot, it's hot!"

Telling Cameron wasn't the same as letting him be involved in making his own decision, and then living with the consequences. That made the lesson crystal clear to him. It's a style of learning that children intuitively comprehend. You don't have to be an adult to understand the value of learning by doing, although there are a lot of adults that still don't get it.

That lesson about the hot coffee may have been over-taught because Cameron doesn't drink coffee *to this day*. Good old Auntie Trish. She's a fan of allowing for a little acting up as well.

PRIDE IN OUR EMPLOYEES' SUCCESS

One of my great joys is seeing my employees succeed and achieve their goals, professionally and personally. It's wonderful, some of the things your employees share with you. Here's an example.

Our Presidents' Council is a regular meeting of the people who report to the presidents of the organization. At one of those meetings, one of the VPs asked me what my next measure of success would look like for our company. I answered, "What would really please me is if everybody who works in our company who wants to own a home can afford to own one."

Near the end of that year, he brought a big present to me during the meeting all wrapped up with big, beautiful gold ribbons on it. It looked like a framed painting or picture. When we unwrapped it, I couldn't believe what I saw. It was a framed collage of smaller pictures of all the employees in that VP's region standing in front of the homes they had bought that year. These were all brand-new homeowners. There must have been a hundred of them.

I lost it. The tears just started flowing down my cheeks, and I lost it.

It still touches at my heart, and I cry tears of joy and pride.

I get so messy. I don't cry pretty at my age. I get snotty and everything. And those were just the pictures from one region of the company.

My call to action to my VPs is that you can't call yourself a leader if you're living in a nice home and your family's well taken care of, but the people you're leading aren't. The following year, I got another frame sent to me for my birthday from a different regional VP. Same thing. Dozens of pictures of employees who were all first-time homeowners.

One of the things about my company that I love so dearly is that the people who report directly to me are also friends. They are really great human beings. They care about each other, about me—and we are *we*. When one of us has an issue, or somebody can't make a flight, the other ones don't hesitate to jump in and support. How do you value that and compensate for that? That goes to culture.

They're all wonderful people. You don't have to be afraid to hug them and tell them, "I love you." You're not going to get a call from HR; you'll get a hug right back. I don't know a lot of CEOs who have that type of relationship with their teams. In that way, I'm really blessed. It's due in part to the culture we've grown but also due to the fact that we hire quality human beings.

SHARE THE WIN

One thing I've long rejected is the idea of one winner. Most often in our society, we think that the winner is the one person who takes home the trophy or gets the prize. The winner gets their face on the Wheaties cereal box. The winner gets the big endorsement deal. The winner gets to ride in the parade. But we don't ever look at what the runners-up get.

Just because somebody else won doesn't mean you lost. Many times, I've won a bid and then gone back to the companies that were second and third and brought them onto my team to help support and deliver. Since they already made it through the other thirty or forty who tried, I figure they must be pretty good. Maybe they didn't get the main contract, maybe they didn't win the big prize, but they still got business. And they learned that customer, so they're ready to compete against me next time. It's smart to think differently about winning and losing.

You don't have to compete *against* each other; you can compete *with* each other.

In my company right now, one of the better ways to get paid is to do what we call splits. In staffing, there are two sides: one side is the job order, and the other is the applicant. A job order is worth so much, and a filled position is worth so much, so you've got different ways to build your commission. We encourage splits, so when a job order comes in, anyone in the company can fill it. No one person, no one office, no one region owns a job order or an applicant. It's a team effort. As a result, we're seeing incomes go up. We're seeing teams work cross-functionally. More importantly, we're fulfilling the needs of more applicants.

The only thing about our policy on splits that surprises me is that it took us a long time to get to that process. People who engage and hustle can earn much better money. I can show you email after email from employees who are super excited about their splits. This again goes to culture—we encourage teamwork instead of just one winner.

I've always thought it would be fun to write a book about the runners-up. Something tells me the finishers in second, third, and fourth place also had pretty good times.

TRANSPARENCY

I strongly believe that the more transparent we become with our knowledge, our vulnerability, our hopes, and our desired outcomes, the more success we will achieve. It's only through transparency that we're able to find solutions.

One of my clients who has a high-level executive position shared something very personal with me about himself. He told me he was gay, but his organization did not know it, and he was scared to tell them. He'd worked there for sixteen years and kept it a secret the entire time.

I asked him why he told me. He said, "I think it's good for you to know this about me. I think that we're going to have a great relationship." His willingness to be transparent was something I appreciated tremendously, and it brought us closer. He's one of my favorite long-time customers, and he's become a friend. My friend doesn't feel the freedom in his company to share this, but he feels free with me. I dislike the situation for him. I honor him for trusting me. Together, we have worked to support change. It's like with my adult children; we're all in a race for humanity. The organizations I invest my personal time with must all support and be about inclusion for all. Period!

In business, I've watched women who openly share their

secrets to success. Whether they do it through mentoring, writing books, or lecturing, the more they share, the more they grow. I'm not saying you should give away the keys to your kingdom. I *am* saying you should keep the streets open in the kingdom. Information flow is vital both ways.

On the other hand, I also know business owners who don't believe in sharing their knowledge. In my industry, there are women who don't want to share what has worked for them for fear they'll give away their secrets to the competition. That's their choice, and I don't judge them for it. However, my belief is that when you share what works or doesn't work, it helps everyone. It keeps economies moving. It promotes your own growth, your innovation, and your best sense of competition. Sharing information is a critical component of any successful corporate culture.

KEY WISDOM AND INSIGHTS

- Seeing coworkers and colleagues as clients and customers is how you begin building a corporate culture.
- Respect and support your employees just as you would in any close, personal relationship.
- Hire great people, then support and develop them to become superstars.
- You don't have to compete *against* each other, you can compete *with* each other.
- The more transparent we become with our knowledge, the more success we will achieve.

CHAPTER NINE

Survive Now, Cry Later

WHEN I WAS IN ENGLAND WITH BERNIE ON OUR third visit, his mom got really sick after a family dinner. She was struggling to breathe. Everyone was panicking and freaking out and wondering what to do. I calmly went over to help her, support her, and keep her comfortable until the emergency responders arrived.

Afterward, Bernie said that it really impressed him that, while everybody else went into a state of uproar and panic, I went into a mode of calm, deliberate action. He thought, "That's somebody I can build a life with."

An important skill, in both business and life, is to learn how to react when something goes horribly wrong. Let's call it the "survive now, cry later" strategy. In other words, stay calm and focused in the difficult moment and keep working until you get through it; you can get upset *afterward*. You'll have time to cry later.

TOMORROW IS ANOTHER DAY

In *Gone with the Wind*, Scarlett O'Hara says, "Tomorrow is another day." I don't claim that calmness is a Southern thing. Still, too many people panic and get distraught in a difficult situation. It's more important to calmly work yourself through it while you're in it. You can let yourself experience all the emotions later. Remind yourself that no matter what happens, tomorrow is another day.

I've seen my share of big presentations turn into mini disasters. If your sales presentation goes south, don't self-destruct in the conference room. You pull yourself together and get through it. You can have a glass of wine and a good cry in the hotel room that evening.

People earn their stripes in the military and in life, not solely because they're bold and not solely because they're strong but, most often, because they're also pragmatic—they're able to manage in the moment toward a goal. They don't get lost or panic when things go wrong.

In business, we get to decide what the battles are. We

can perform strategically and with intensity during the battle, then pick our own moments later to come back and decompress.

RESILIENCE IS REQUIRED

One of the most important qualities for a successful career in business is resilience. There will be setbacks. You will suffer defeats. You will get knocked down, lose big deals, suffer injustice, and be blamed for things that were not your fault. It's part of business and life.

For example, it's not fun for me to know that potential clients or competitors may see me first as a woman or a minority. I don't see myself that way, and neither should they. While being a woman entrepreneur framed opportunity for me, I never let it put borders around my determination or my resilience. The best part about winning the battle against discrimination, or against any defeat, is that it removes mountains for others.

OVERCOMING OBSTACLES

I've found that most people I meet have overcome some significant obstacle, hardship, or crisis in their lives. It could be the loss of a loved one, a divorce, a failed business, a legal matter, or a medical diagnosis. Or maybe it's something more deeply personal from childhood.

In my case, I've already told you that I grew up in the segregated South, had a teacher and classmates who used the n-word in school, and lost my father when I was a young woman. But there's another very personal setback I want to mention, as well. Many of us care about how we look; it's why we groom ourselves and wear makeup, right? Well, this setback was a physical accident that left my face disfigured.

As a successful female entrepreneur and business leader, I am frequently asked to appear on television shows, cable news programs, or to do live presentations or on-camera interviews. It's something I enjoy. So when the accident disfigured my face, it was a serious blow to me, both personally and professionally.

I was on a commercial flight on a major airline. The plane had pulled up to the gate and stopped. "Ding. Welcome to Los Angeles. You are now free to move about the cabin. Be careful when opening the overhead bins as objects may have shifted in flight."

If I could only go back in time to that moment.

The man across the aisle from me stood up and began to remove his heavy carry-on bag from the overhead compartment. Just as he lifted it up, the plane lurched forward. I saw a dark blur coming toward my face really fast. Too fast for me to move. Then *boom*. Bright light. I felt like I had been punched in the face by Mike Tyson. Or kicked by a horse. The next thing I knew I was on the floor of the airplane wondering what had happened.

When I regained my composure I stood up. Everyone was staring at me. People were asking me if I was okay. I remember my face was stinging and hurting really bad. It had been a hard thump right to the front of my face.

My brother Carlton was horrified. He said, "Sister, let me see. Let me see."

I said, "Get me to the bathroom. Just get me to the bathroom."

We sprinted off the plane. Walking through the terminal on the way to the bathroom, I noticed I had a chipped tooth and I was bleeding. When I got to the ladies' room, the first thing I did was look in the mirror. Oh no.

I wanted to get out of there as fast as possible. I just remember being in the car and merging onto the 405 freeway toward Palos Verdes. I looked in the mirror again. I said, "I better go to the doctor. I better go to the doctor. Now."

I CAN'T LET PEOPLE SEE ME LIKE THIS

I was scheduled to be a guest speaker the next day to a large audience at NBC. It had been set up weeks in advance. I called my contact at NBC, Marcia, and told her what happened. I asked her if it would be okay if I sent someone else to give the speech. She knew Carlton really well, so I was hoping he could take my place. Marcia said, "No, Janice. They're all coming here to see you, sweetheart."

I tried again to explain to Marcia what my face looked like and how swollen I was. She said, "Janice, it's up to you. You make the choice." I thought about it. I decided I was going to go and give the presentation. But I told Marcia, "Just meet me before the presentation and look at my face. I just need to make sure it's okay for your audience."

When Marcia saw me, she gasped. She didn't know what to say. I assume it was worse than she expected. Maybe she thought I was exaggerating when I described how my face looked over the phone the day before.

After seeing me, she thought it was incredibly brave and admirable that I showed up to fulfill my commitment. I said, "Marcia, this is Hollywood after all. If you're okay with it, I'll just put on my big sunglasses and keep them on." That's how I made the presentation. Marcia is a dear, dear friend. She was so smart to insist that I at least show up, and she supported my decision to suffer through the pain that day. From her, I've learned so much, and I feel blessed that the lady who is so much smarter than I am continues our friendship to this day.

Meanwhile, my daughter began researching doctors. She said, "Mom, you really need to go see someone."

There was another issue on the horizon. In two weeks, I was supposed to do a big TV news appearance in London. I was more worried about doing TV than giving a speech, as TV cameras zoom in close and broadcast your face into millions of homes.

I was fearful of how I would be received by viewers. But then my son Brett said something I'll never forget. He said, "Mom, if you think people are paying more attention to what's outside your head than what's inside your head, maybe you've got the problem." So I went and I did the TV show. Now that video clip is out there on the Internet, and truth be told, I do look really beat up.

But it was very empowering for me. The network got a lot of positive feedback from that show, and despite my fears, I was able to deliver a solid interview. I got past that point of insecurity. Had I been a man, I don't think I would have had such issues around my appearance—I've seen some scary-looking men regularly delivering the news!

CURING THE PAIN

Just before the accident, I had been meeting with television producers who were interested in designing a TV series around me. But now my face was disfigured. The offers for TV shows evaporated.

I looked into having facial surgery, but the surgeon said there was a 50 percent chance that I'd be worse off after the surgery. I sulked about the decision for three days, but I was in so much pain, the surgery was a risk I was prepared to take.

Perhaps what bothered me most was that it hurt to laugh. That was hard for me because I'm a laugher. My daughter, Kay, said, "Mom, you can't be in pain when you laugh. Laughter is a joy pill. We've got to figure out what to do."

Instead of doing surgery right away, I let Kay take me to Dr. John Kim, who is a Korean acupuncturist a block away from the beach. Step one, he said, was to get rid of the pain. Within twenty minutes of him sticking needles in me, the pain actually subsided. It blew my mind. I had been in pain for weeks, and he gave me my miracle within minutes. Dr. Kim said, "Let me work with you for six weeks and see if we can make the pain go away permanently."

He felt that, with further treatment, he could get the shape and movement back in my face. He had identified where the nerve damage was. Within six weeks, I noticed a remarkable difference in how I looked. I was sold. I stayed with Dr. Kim for about eight months. He got me to the point where I was out of pain and almost recovered.

After the accident and prior to my treatment with Dr. Kim, I was so disfigured I would scare children. He got me past that. I was thrilled to avoid the risk of facial surgery. Dr. Kim also gave me great spiritual support, and I will treasure him forever for his beautiful spirit and immaculate skill.

The experience of having that accident, overcoming it, growing beyond it, and not letting it stop me was really affirming. Rather than teach me something new, it affirmed what I had always believed. When our children were young, Bernie and I would tell them, "You can do anything you put your mind to." This experience reproved that to me. And I am grateful for it. From time to time, or from certain angles, the damage to my facial muscles is still evident. But that's a small price to pay for having regained and gained so much.

As with any setback in life you might call unlucky or sad, it puts you in touch with who you are. As the great Albert Einstein said, "Adversity introduces a man to himself." What I'm certain old Albert meant was, "Adversity introduces a man *or woman* to himself *or herself.*" But he was a smart dude.

WHEN TO STEP ON THE GAS PEDAL

In nearly forty years as a business owner, I've been through more economic cycles than I can count on two hands. Economic boom followed by bust followed by yet another boom. But the last downturn in 2008 was by far the worst.

Many business owners learned some tough lessons during the Great Recession. Thousands of companies failed or barely survived. We saw several of our competitors go under. My company weathered the storm remarkably well, and we even grew in some areas. That's because we operate under a different philosophy than most companies.

I'm sure you've heard the saying, "When the going gets tough, the tough get going." It means that when life gets difficult, people will usually step up and work even harder to make it through. While there's nothing wrong with buckling down in times of hardship, I prefer a different strategy.

I think the saying should be, "When everything is going great, that's the time to work even harder." I believe when business is good, growth is strong, customers are happy, and everyone is making money, that's the time to step on the gas pedal. That's the time to forge ahead. That's the time to assess your weaknesses and areas that are in need of improvement. There is great value in getting out in front of problems before they happen.

But when the US economy was booming before the recession, a lot of business owners took their foot off the gas. They decided to coast a little bit. They made the classic entrepreneurial mistake—they got cocky. Their philosophy was, "We've had back-to-back-to-back growth years, it's going to continue, so why not kick back and relax."

At my company, we didn't do that. In Chapter 7, I shared with you one of Bernie's favorite quotes: "When is the best time to tell your wife you love her? Before someone else does." That is the very basis of what we believe. We don't wait until something bad happens to take action. When times are good, we step on the gas pedal. So when the recession hit, our company was much better prepared to battle adversity.

I really believe this was proof of what I thought to be true all along: work like crazy when it's good, and you'll be in a better position when it's bad. People who know me personally sometimes say, "Why is Janice so hell-bent on building that or growing this?" It's because I believe in always working today as if it's your last day to get it done. This philosophy keeps you sharp and excited and always marching forward.

A true leader, a true entrepreneur is constantly on the lookout for ways to improve, grow, and expand, *especially* during times of great prosperity. They are looking for ways to continuously act up. Then in the lean years that follow the boom years, as they always do, they don't suffer as much.

HEAR ME ROAR

In 1971, recording artist Helen Reddy enjoyed a hit song titled "I Am Woman." The lyrics proclaimed the strength of women succeeding in a man's world. The self-proclaimed Godfather of Soul, James Brown, enjoyed his own hit on the topic with a song titled "It's a Man's World." He, too, acknowledged that with all the achievements men take credit for, none would exist without the support of women.

The discussion of man vs. woman has existed since life began. Did Eve really get her existence from Adam's rib? Did she repay the favor by tempting him with an apple and causing him to know his first failure? Regardless, there is no human race without the fairer sex.

If you *wish* for success, you *could* achieve it. If you *hope* for success you *might* achieve it. But if you *decide* to work intelligently and take advantage of all the opportunities available to you, you *will* achieve it.

—BERNIE

The battle of the sexes may continue to cause harm, or create foreplay, depending on your perspective, but I believe the emotional strengths and needs of people are not gender-based. I've known men who cry at sad movies and women who are tough as nails. Former prime minister of Britain, Margaret Thatcher, was so tough, she earned the nickname "The Iron Lady."

Perpetuating gender compliments can creep into defending gender bias. In business, the human brain and emotional power of leadership must support multigendered opportunity and success. Crediting one gender or the other with better skill, resilience, or intuition leans toward suggesting that one gender might be better at leadership. What women do well, often by necessity, is that they learn to become Superwoman in Superman's world.

ETHICS VS. LAWS

According to a recent global survey, the majority of people in powerful positions stated that they will cheat if they don't think they will get caught. Business owners I've talked with will sometimes even admit this; if they know they can get away with it, they'll behave unethically.

Ethics and laws aren't the same things, no matter how much we might wish they were.

It's not for me to judge or label other companies and their ethical practices. But I can think of a number of situations where clients weren't ethical in how they worked with me, even if what they did was technically legal. In some cases, it just comes down to who has the best lawyer or the largest legal purse. So you have to be smart about the law, and you have to be clear and determined about what your ethical standards are. You have to know how to mitigate negative legal entanglements.

Years ago, we were working to win the business of a potential client in North Carolina. Their factory was near my hometown. I really wanted to win the business so we could create jobs and economic vitality in the region where I grew up.

My sister, Trish, did some research on the company and found out that their reputation was not good. Trish told me that the company is known for moving around a lot (which is always a red flag), they have lots of workers' comp injuries, and they paid employees a low wage. Sometimes companies put temporary staff in working conditions that may not be the safest, healthiest environments, and apparently, this company made a habit of doing that.

But the company was going to pay us really well for our services. We weren't providing people; we were providing technology and process. It would have been a very valuable account for us to have.

I thought about it for a while. I tried to justify taking on this company by telling myself, "We can do good with that money." The old Robin Hood rationalization. The business would have helped us penetrate the Southeastern United States.

In the end, after much soul searching, we walked away from it. Ultimately, we determined that working with a company like that does not align with our own values as a company or as individuals. From then on, I decided that I would not do business with any company where I would not send one of my own family members to work. I've lived by that principle ever since.

I don't know if I won by walking away from that

business. As an ethical individual, it felt great. But as a businessperson, one could argue that it was my responsibility to work with that client. After all, my employees rely on me to grow and expand the business. If we were a public company, we would most likely *have had to* take that business; our shareholders would demand it. You're not always going to know a company's standards or practices before you engage, but you can—and must—always do your diligence once such is discovered.

Life and business are full of gray areas with infinite shades. There are often no right answers, only choices that we make and then have to live with. I'm sure if I investigated many of the companies we do business with, there would be moral questions. Mama used to say, "Human beings are perfect creatures with imperfections." Maybe businesses are too—perfect communities coalesced around perfect ideals but with imperfections.

KEY WISDOM AND INSIGHTS

- Survive now, cry later. Always stay calm and focused in a difficult moment until you get through it; you can get upset afterward.
- Tomorrow is another day. Everyone makes mistakes, so when you do, accept it, learn from it, and vow to do better tomorrow.

- Adversity puts you in touch with who you really are. Struggle builds character.
- When everything is going great, that's the time to work even harder.
- Ethics and law aren't the same things, no matter how much we might wish they were. In business, eventually you will run into people and companies with questionable ethics. Stay true to yourself and your values.

❖

CHAPTER TEN

Until We Win

I'VE NEVER BEEN THAT GORGEOUS PERSON WHO people stared at or were going to harass sexually. I don't know that experience, thank God. But I have experienced gender bias, which can feel like sexual harassment to some degree. A lot has changed for women in the forty years since I began as an entrepreneur. But a lot still needs to change.

OVERCOME THE OPPORTUNITY GAP

As we all know, a significant wage gap still exists between men and women who work in similar jobs. From my perspective, not from any in-depth study or data-supported knowledge across industries, I believe that the disparity in pay between men and women is aligned with the disparity in the opportunity for access to information.

Historically, women have not been included in the information processes of building businesses, and it doesn't matter what that business is. It can be producing a movie or building a rocket; women have not been in that inner circle of information. Some refer to this as the old boys' network.

When you don't know what's going on, you don't know what to ask. You don't know what your value is. This is why I stress that it is important to ask the right questions, then listen for the right answers.

The business of Hollywood, where movie stars have agents who negotiate their pay, is not something I know well, but in our company, we are agents for the applicants when we are speaking with companies. It's on us to ask those important questions and to make sure we're not only giving those clients the best talent at the best cost but giving employees the best opportunities for the best wages.

The absence of information breeds poor performance. What's worse, that performance may not necessarily be how someone actually delivers their work as much as how they are credited for that work and, as a result, how they're compensated for that work. So for me, the answer is very simple. It is the absence of information that allows people to either be treated poorly or to accept poor treatment. When you don't know your worth, you don't know your value.

That gender pay gap needs to be closed once and for all. But there is an even more important gap that isn't talked about much. It's the *opportunity gap* between the genders.

The vast majority of CEOs and high-level executives are white men. Women still are not getting the opportunity to join the C-suite in the same numbers men are. And only a small fraction of the startup companies that receive venture capital funding each year are woman-owned. Never mind the pay gap, women just aren't getting the same opportunities men are. I make it my business to engage with organizations and people who work to break down barriers and create opportunities for all.

AVOIDING SEXUAL HARASSMENT

We don't need to look too far today to see that mishandling sexual harassment claims can wreak havoc on an organization. The stakes are very high for turning a blind eye to issues that we know are occurring, whether someone is speaking up or not. It is important for us to be good stewards of good behavior. As leaders in our businesses, or owners of our businesses, that means that we have to make sure that everyone in the organization is very clear on what is sexual harassment and what is not, and what is good behavior and what is not.

It's no new news to most women in business that sexual harassment has been an area of concern for some time. We can even see it evidenced and celebrated in certain movies or in music that we can handily recall. So when it comes to how sexual harassment is playing out in the news today, very few women are surprised at this. However, it's really important that we understand that while the focus is on where women are with respect to men in power, the truth is that if you are a woman business leader or business owner, you face that same risk if you're in the power seat.

What is that risk? It's the risk of not understanding what's okay, and what's not okay. Much of the attention today is given to very large organizations that historically have not had women in top leadership roles. But when you're starting your own business, you're at the top, so you need to have very clear protocols that are specific to you and your company.

Sexual harassment is not gender specific. It can occur most often from positions of power plays, not gender plays. So it's really important for us to understand where our employees are culturally with us, and with each other. Often in small businesses, friendship can become a very blurry line, and comments or actions can be misunderstood very easily.

So it makes good sense for you as a business owner, no matter how many employees you have, even if it's just you and one other employee, to understand the rules and the guidelines around sexual harassment and make sure that you allow everyone to be comfortable. The truth is that many, many terrific contributions from employees have been lost by people feeling that they've been harassed, or actually having been harassed, and not feeling therefore free to stay with the company or to continue to contribute their best work.

We want everyone to be able to bring their full selves to work, and that means that they have to be treated with respect and have their boundaries respected as well. When we have an organization that allows people to feel safe, to work however they can best perform within the guidelines of our organization, we have an organization that's better poised for growth. We have an organization where employees enjoy the work they do better, and we have an organization where when the going gets tough, people can plow in, and they don't have those negative feelings of not being appreciated or respected that they so very much desire and deserve.

Sexual harassment is an illness in an organization if it's

allowed to occur. So we also want an organization where people can see it is not tolerated, therefore they feel free to speak up when they sense something happening that shouldn't be. We should also be vigilant at the time we hire someone that their rights in this regard are made clear to them by whoever the hiring person is.

If you are an employee in a company, no matter what your ranking is in that organization, if you begin to perceive that you're being discriminated against because of your gender or for any reason, it is very important that you read the law, understand what your rights are, and then you speak appropriately to those in a position of authority. It's never a good idea to let something simmer or go unreported. It's always best to speak openly. Understand that doesn't mean you're always right in your perception, but you do always have the right to speak your perception. But first, learn what the rules really are and how you're performing within them.

No one should sustain seeing what they believe is unfair treatment occur whether it's in form of sexual harassment or a discrimination of any sort. At the end of the day, you own the right to speak up when you think that you're not being treated fairly or legally. You should first educate yourself as best you can on what your rights are, and once you've had the proper discussion with the appropriate people in the organization, then make the decision that is best for you.

For many business owners, especially startups and small businesses, this area becomes multifaceted because not only are you now in the seat of responsibility for how your employees are being treated, and how they are receiving appropriate education in protocols and requirements, you also very often may be seeking opportunities or doing business with companies who may not respect you, based on your gender or any other reason. So knowing your rights and how best to voice those to a client becomes critical to the success of your business. Regardless of whether you have one employee or hundreds of employees, depending on the decisions you make and the actions you take, you still need to know what your rights are as a business.

There are very few countries you will do business in where there are not some regulations around how businesses treat each other and their employees. Whether that is about inclusiveness, or whether that's a regulatory requirement, it still is important for you to understand the dynamics that are present in any country in which you do business. One of the best things that a business can do, regardless of size, is to join organizations that support and ensure that the education around women-owned businesses or minority-owned businesses is occurring.

Some of the organizations I have mentioned enjoying membership in for many years include, the Women's

Business Enterprise National Council (WBENC), the National Minority Supplier Development Council (NMSDC), Women Presidents and Owners (WPO), the Women's Business Enterprise Council (WBEC), the National LGBT Chamber of Commerce (NGLCC) and Harvard Women's Leadership Board (WLB). Another great organization is the National Utilities Development Council (NUDC). These organizations all have within their charter tremendous information that helps to educate you around business and your rights in business. These organizations also advocate for corporate contracting, and they are excellent for networking. So no matter where you are, if you're starting a business, these are great ones to be a member of.

One other one that you should consider is WeConnect. WeConnect is an international organization of women business owners and corporations that do business with them across the globe. These organizations are very often looked at as vehicles for gaining access to corporate contracts, but they are more valuable for access to information.

They also offer seminars that can help you with timely education on different areas that pertain to business, whether it's how to do business taxes or new regulations coming out that might impact your business, or any number of ways to grow your business. They are great networking forums, and an investment of time in any of these organizations is a worthwhile investment for your company.

MULTICULTURAL AWARENESS

The conversations on access and equality are happening in various spaces and various ways all over the world today. If you're in business leadership at any level, but particularly if you're a business owner, it's important to understand and listen to what's going on in this area. More importantly, your goal is to make sure that if your company becomes part of the conversation, it's being discussed as an example of the right way to do things. Lots of this is considered common sense, but common sense isn't that common anymore.

When we cross cultures, for example, by doing business in another country, what is right in one culture may be perceived as something completely disrespectful or unacceptable in another culture. So if you're going to do business across country lines, or across culture lines, make sure you understand the regulations and norms for the cultural practices where you're going to do business so that you can be thoughtful and respectful in accordance with those cultures.

Your business brand that you build may be known for one

core thing across the globe, but locale by locale, you're going to be known for how you're treating those local customers and employees. That is something that can make or break your business. It's important to understand, to know about, and whenever possible, to hire people locally so that they can position you in the best advantage in that marketplace.

STARTING SALARIES MATTER

Starting salaries matter a lot. They dictate how you're paid as you progress up through an organization. When you're applying for a job, that employer will want to know your current salary, and that will often be the basis for your new salary. So it's important to negotiate for the highest starting salary possible every time you join a new company.

When you interview for a job, the best thing you can do is study that company to learn about their pay and benefits. There are reviews written by employees for most major employers online on sites like Glassdoor.com. Try to figure out what the salary range is for the position you're applying for, and then negotiate for the high end. If you are a business owner, please remember this as you schedule for hiring.

It's perfectly acceptable to ask the hiring manager or HR

representative about their corporate culture, compensation range, and employment practices. I also think it's fair game to ask them at the point you receive an offer whether the salary offer is the same that everybody else gets for this position. It's better to find out before you accept an offer. Otherwise, you may be hired at one salary only to find out later that men doing the exact same job in the same location are paid significantly more.

Likewise, if you're an entrepreneur, a business owner, or are in a position to hire employees, I believe you have an obligation to make sure you're being fair to the genders in hiring, compensation, and promotions within your organization. Hiring managers have a responsibility to eliminate both the wage gap *and* the opportunity gap.

HUMAN RESOURCES CAN MAKE OR BREAK A COMPANY

I love attending seminars and conferences where I can hear from other business leaders in a wide range of industries. I especially enjoy when a titan of industry shares some unexpected twist on an accepted principle or reveals something that they believe has attributed to their success.

Jack Welch, chairman and CEO of General Electric from 1981 to 2001, is one such example. He's known as one of the all-time great chief executives in the history of global business. During his reign as CEO, GE's stock rose by 4,000 percent. His personal net worth is estimated at $750 million. And upon retiring from the company, he received a severance payment of $417 million. Clearly, this is a man who understood business and finance. I've met some of his mentees who have gone on to great business leadership success on their own.

MAMA SAYS
EDUCATION IS FREEDOM

As I said in the beginning of this book, I attended a segregated school until eleventh grade. With my mom and dad as teachers and role models, we never shied away from how hard things were, but we focused on how *possible* things were. They were possible through education for us. Daddy would say, "You can learn from everybody, and anybody you can't learn from is your problem, not theirs."

My dad believed that educated people had more choices. The phrase "Education is freedom" was right up on our wall alongside the pictures of Martin Luther King, John Kennedy, and Jesus Christ. It was religion in our house to do your homework before you did anything else when you got home from school.

My dad would say, "Education is freedom." My mom would say, "Information is power." I taught my children those truths as well. To this day, if you ask my wonderfully accomplished adult children, "Education is?" They'll complete the sentence, "Freedom."

Now, most of the CEOs whom I've read about or spoken with seem to most highly value their chief financial officer. The CFO is the money guy at a company. But Jack Welch had a different take. I was fortunate enough to take a two-day class with Jack. He told me that while most CEOs look to have their CFO in their hip pocket, he believed you should have the chief human resources officer in your hip pocket. He said HR is the one department that has the potential to make the greatest difference in your organization by finding, recruiting, compensating, and retaining top talent in all areas of the company.

That made perfect sense to me. Being in the staffing business, I've seen the difference HR can make at a company—especially with engineers and technical employees, but it's true in every part of the company.

HIRING FIRST EMPLOYEES

When many entrepreneurs start their first business, they are the only employee for quite a while. Hence, the entrepreneur is the most important employee of the company. Gradually the entrepreneur will begin to hire freelancers, and maybe a few family members to work part-time. But the day you hire your first full-time employee, you are no longer the key employee. Your employees are your most important internal customers. They should be treated appropriately.

Most business owners tend to hire in their own image. They hire people who they think they'd like to work with. That's a mistake that too many entrepreneurs make. If we hire employees just like us, in our image, then we're not adding anything new to the talent roster. It makes great sense to hire people we'd most enjoy working for, not just with.

If you're the company founder and you're a techie coder who lives on GitHub, then don't hire another nerdy coder just like yourself. That won't expand your company's talent pool. Instead, hire a smart salesperson who wears appropriate suits and loves enjoying time with clients over sushi. Or hire a colorful creative type who can write dynamite copy and edit video for viral ad campaigns.

When I sit in a meeting, if somebody's just going to repeat what I said and think what I think, it's wasted space. It's wasted time. When we engage in sales presentations, I tell my teams not to say, "I agree with what Janice said." That's really not helpful because I've already said it.

Instead, take the conversation forward to something new. Something important. Something elevating. Some new topic that will add value to the client. Don't just nod approval and repeat what someone else already said.

I learned much later in my career that I don't have to

like all the people I work with. I do have to like the *way* they work and the outcomes they deliver. But we don't need to hang out together. In fact, if I had to pull teams together in order to meet specific outcomes, most likely, that team would not be comprised of people I want to lounge around the pool with on a weekend. While the business leaders across my organization are all people I enjoy, the full teams are wonderfully diverse in every possible way.

WORK WILL CONTINUE TO REDEFINE ITSELF

Automation, artificial intelligence, virtual reality, augmented reality. In my opinion, the rapid advances in AI technology do not mean that in the future, fewer people will work because robots are doing our jobs. It means that workers will have to be educated or retrained to operate alongside these new technologies. As technology advances, work will continue to redefine itself.

Before Henry Ford began mass producing automobiles, we didn't need auto mechanics. But once automobiles took over as the primary means of transportation in America, mechanics were in high demand. The craftsmen who specialized in building stagecoaches and horse carriages had to learn new skills. New technologies create new jobs, but those jobs require different skillsets.

One of my good friends who oversees HR for a major public utility currently has more than two hundred job openings. We're working with her to write job descriptions for them. Many go unfilled because they require new skills that currently are hard to find in the workforce. There are open positions waiting to be filled, but the applicants aren't fitted to the work.

It's a similar story with computing science and writing code. There are so many open jobs that talented coders can basically set their own price because not enough people know how to code. When I hear people say, "I can't find a job." I tell them, "You're just looking in the wrong place, *from* the wrong place."

BEING THOUGHTFUL ISN'T THE SAME AS THINKING

In our company, we share a book with our employees titled *As a Person Thinks*. When the book was originally published, the title was *As a Man Thinketh*. But I got the rights and changed it.

The book has a powerful message. Your thoughts aren't just indicators of what's going on in your life at the present time. They are also *generators* of what *will* happen in your life in the future. I believe in that process. I think and visualize what I want to happen. I do it regularly.

I deliberately experience things in my mind before they actually happen in reality. This has a number of benefits. First, it helps me to mitigate risk because I mentally walk through what I want to happen, and in so doing, I notice potential pitfalls. Second, since I feel the feelings of it happening in my mind, I'm comfortable with it when it actually occurs. I *expect* it to happen.

The value of focused thought is underrated. Many people try to ignore or run away from their thoughts. Or they think about negative outcomes. "I don't think this is going to work. I'll never land that big account." Sometimes your thoughts are the purest conversation you can have. Don't let them be negative or self-destructive. That's my belief, and it may sound crazy to some. Still, it's a technique that has worked for me time and again.

THE RESULT IS THE TRUTH

The most expensive picture frame I have is very small. It

sits on one of my office desks. There is no picture in it. It simply has words I wrote: "The result is the truth." You will reveal how well-suited you are for any given task by the results you achieve. This rule applies to all areas of business, and it deserves the frame it's in!

For example, here's a question I get from time to time. "How do I know whether I'm better suited to be an employee or an entrepreneur?"

My answer is, "The result is the truth."

As a business owner, your income and the company's success are two good indicators of your result. If you've launched a successful startup that earned profit and you loved every minute of it, that's your result. That's your truth. You're well-suited to entrepreneurship.

But if you've failed at several startup companies, hated every minute of it, and you dread the thought of doing it again, that's a pretty clear result. That's your truth. Maybe entrepreneurship isn't for you.

Or if you've been miserable as an employee and you get unsatisfactory job evaluations year after year, that's also a clear result. That's your truth. Maybe you'd do much better working for yourself.

In order to be a good employee, you follow rules and you get measured. Your bosses and supervisors are going to help you define whether you're a good employee. In most companies that sort of communication is clear. That's your result.

DON'T BE AFRAID TO DO SOMETHING ELSE

I was in Atlanta recently, participating in a panel at a career conference. Hundreds of millennials were in the audience. One young woman stood at the microphone and asked, "I'm in sales, and I work really hard, but I'm just not getting results. What am I doing wrong?" Several of the panelists offered advice such as, "Work smart, not hard," and, "Get proper sales training." But the young woman insisted that she's tried everything, and no matter what she does, the results just aren't there.

The other panelists were all attempting to be supportive in helping find her missing link in sales. But I wouldn't. In my mind, I was thinking, "The result is the truth." I blurted out, "It sounds like you're just not right for the industry. That role is not right for you. Do something else."

The room fell silent. There was an awkward moment. The other panelists looked at me with faces that suggested I should walk it back and say something encouraging. I didn't. Then everyone realized I was right, and the whole room laughed. Later, the young woman wrote me an engaging thank-you note. She had discovered her passion elsewhere and today continues on her road to success.

Sometimes that's the correct answer. Do something else.

If you've tried your best at a certain career or business but the results just aren't there, don't be afraid to do something else. That's not career advice you hear very often. It takes boldness for me to say it. But it's the truth. You didn't buy this book for me to whitewash reality for you.

The result is the truth.

There's absolutely no shame in figuring out that a particular career you ended up in may not be the one ideally suited to your strengths. In fact, figuring that out early is a great thing. It can save you years of struggle and anxiety. It's far better to move away from something that's not working for you so you can move toward finding what you're truly good at.

In the conclusion to this book, I'll share a few thoughts on finding what you're passionate about and, hence, what you'll succeed at.

KEY WISDOM AND INSIGHTS

- Starting salaries matter a lot because future raises and job offers will likely be based on that starting salary.
- Human resources can make or break a company by the quality of the talent they recruit and retain.
- If you can't find a job, you're looking in the wrong place. The jobs openings are there, but you may need to develop new skills.

- The result is the truth. If you're working hard but the results are not coming, maybe you're in the wrong position.
- Don't be afraid to do something else. Life is too short to grind away at something you're either not good at or don't enjoy.

Conclusion

Know Your Ministry

ONE OF THE COMMON TAGLINES THAT WE REPEAT throughout our company-wide training materials is, "Everything matters." What we mean is that everything you do as an employee, as a business owner, as a salesperson, as a parent, or as an entrepreneur may be noticed by and/or impact others. You've heard the old saying that if you tell one person, then eventually ten other people will know. Business is like that.

I don't think a lot of entrepreneurs step back to fully comprehend how small certain communities are in the business world. If you treat one client poorly, they're going to talk to other companies in that industry. And before you know it, you've been labeled with a bad reputation, whether it's deserved it or not.

On the other hand, if you operate under the philosophy of everything matters, your clients are going to spread the word that you're a top-quality organization. They're going to recommend you and refer clients to you. They may not even tell you they're doing it.

This lesson really came to life for me at an energy industry conference I attended. I was sitting in the audience listening to a panel of utility company CEOs take questions about the industry. One person stood up and asked, "How is it that you hit the mark and win every year with your diversity supplier?"

The CEO who fielded the question was one of our clients. She said, "Well, the answer is sitting right there among you in the audience." She called out my company's name and mentioned how we continue to be a reliable and innovative workforce solutions partner for them year after year. I had no idea she was going to single us out, let alone give us such a tremendous compliment. I was smiling from ear to ear.

After that session, dozens of potential customers were coming up to me asking for my business card. That is the power of reputation and reference. The CEO was aware of the great job we were doing for her. And then she told everyone in the room about us. Just like Mama used to say, "It's not what you say about yourself, it's what other people say about you that has the most impact." Everything matters. So I'll say this about the CEO. She is one of my sheroes!

YOU DON'T HAVE TO BE A SUPER-SHERO

Often, I've been a shero. However, early in my career as a business owner, I noticed myself trying to be everything to everybody. I wanted to be a super-shero who could leap tall buildings. I would fly around Gotham helping everyone who asked for my help.

Eventually, it was too much. I had to accept that at the end of the day, when I take the cape and stilettos off, I'm just a mere mortal. Something had to be left over for my family and me. But I didn't know what to say yes to and what to say no to.

My spiritual advisor, Reverend Jay Armstrong, is a man I admire tremendously. He always gives me wise counsel. Even more, he helps me think about things in a different way.

Reverend Jay helped me think through my desire to be a super-shero. He said, "The important thing in life is to know your ministry. Your ministry isn't to work long hours so you can give every person whatever they ask for. Your ministry is what *you* are passionate about. Once you identify your ministry, then you can passionately give where you care about. Giving with passion to one or two things is more powerful than giving to many things just out of obligation." This made perfect sense to me.

I could have become so busy being a shero to everyone that I couldn't focus on what was most important to me, my business and my family. If you're in business, your first responsibility is to that business. If you're not expanding, satisfying your customers, and serving your employees, then that's a signal that you need to work more *inside* that business. I realized that my ministry was my business and all of its employees.

I also use Reverend Jay's advice to decide which charities and nonprofits I support. We get bombarded by hundreds of requests each year from charities. They're all worthwhile. But we can't support them all. Luckily, I know my ministry.

I'm passionate about education. So any education-related requests that come in, we will look at, and then we vet from there. That enables me to eliminate a lot of requests from my personal agenda, even though it doesn't mean that I don't care about those others.

YOUR PASSION WILL COME TO YOU

I knew when I was very young that I wanted to do good. That desire came more from the political economy than the church I worshiped in. But it took me years to figure out exactly *how* I wanted to do good and the *best* way I could help the world. The process of identifying where my humanitarian efforts would lie happened for me over time.

Reverend Jay Armstrong once said to me, "You don't have to search for your ministry, it will come to you when you're ready if you live on the path of doing good as you do well."

MAMA SAYS
LET YOUR DREAMS BUILD YOUR PURPOSE

When I was a teenager, my siblings called me a daydreamer. I would tell my mom all the stuff I was dreaming about in Sunday school. This led to one of the few times I saw my mother disappointed to the point of frustration. She said to me, "You come up with all of these great ideas and big dreams, but then you don't follow through on them. Why don't you write down those dreams and then figure out a plan for how you're going to make them happen. Whatever you're dreaming about, make it your purpose. Then you'll stay focused on it and make it happen." Mama was, and still is, right. I wrote a lot about ActOne before day one of its existence.

I encourage people just to be open and listen. When your life purpose comes to you, I don't think it comes as a whisper. I don't think you're going to miss it if you're busy. If you're paying attention to how you live and what you're doing, it will happen naturally. One day, you'll discover where you will make your imprint on the world and how you will do your good thing. Then, for the rest of your life, you'll know your ministry.

You can immediately tell the difference between someone who is passionately committed and someone who is just going through the motions. People who are passionately committed have identified their ministry, and they know what they have to offer the world. It's the thing they will do regardless.

MY WISH FOR YOU

Many of us eventually find ourselves asking the question, "What do I do with all of this? I've built a career, so what? What now?" It's a common question. The answer lies in that ministry—that good thing that each of us must identify for ourselves. That's what we do with all of this.

And that is my wish for you as you build your career and your life. When you find your ministry, focus on it with passion. Then maybe when you get to be my age, you too will be asked to write a book and share your wisdom forward.

God Bless you, and thank you for reading this book. If you believe any of it, live it. Go act up!

—JANICE

Acknowledgments

WHILE I THANK EVERYTHING AND EVERYONE FOR the tremendous life journey I'm enjoying that fuels the content of this book, there are those without whom this book would be void. They are:

Mom and Dad, for being everything I would seek to become and for living what love looks like!

Sister, Sandy, and all siblings—Sandy welcomed me to a new life in California and supported every one of my dreams, as have my siblings who continue to work with me and keep Mommie and Dad's dreams for us alive!

Husband Bernie, for seeing me as beautiful when I saw "less than," and for believing...unconditionally.

Children, Kay and Brett, for inspiring me to be my best self, 24/7 and for teaching me the truth of "When you're green, you grow. When you're ripe, you rot."

ActOne Group family who, every day, honors our credo of FEET—Freedom to innovate, Excellence in delivery, because Everything matters, invest the Time to understand...and for keeping our candidates the center of our universe!

My brother Carlton, specifically, for knowing and loving me in a timely, most relevant way—day to day! In this spirit, I add Linda, Patricia, and John. Tina, my niece, has been a sister/daughter along this journey and continues to be so!

Gwen Moore, who boldly scolded me into certifying my organization as a minority/woman-owned firm when I insisted that great service should be enough.

For all the work done for all the right reasons, I thank Pam and my WBENC family; Elizabeth, Michael, and my WeConnect family; Harriet Michel and NMSDC forever; Marsha and WPO; and Mayank and MSDUK.

For love and learning, I thank NCA&T and Aggies everywhere!

Nathan Pettijohn, whose belief, passion, brilliance, and dedication to our cause steered me back to loving the purpose and delivery of this book.

About the Author

JANICE BRYANT HOWROYD, a North Carolina native, left her hometown in 1976 armed with $900. Two years later she founded ActOne, which she grew into a multibillion-dollar global organization that now leads the human resources industry. With 2,000+ employees across more than twenty countries, ActOne Group is the largest privately held, woman-owned workforce solutions company in the world. A businesswoman, entrepreneur, educator, and ambassador, Janice has also worked with U.S. presidents Bill Clinton, George W. Bush, and Barack Obama. In 2016 she was appointed by President Obama as an advisor on HBCUs (Historically Black Colleges and Universities), and continues her service. Her passion for education, mentorship, and self-empowerment initiatives has earned her extensive professional and philanthropic recognition. Her passion to support women and next generations in achieving their dreams of self-fulfillment are key motivators to her sharing her story.